THE
American
Bartenders School
GUIDE TO
DRINKS

THE American Bartenders School GUIDE TO DRINKS

by Jack Tiano

SMITHMARK

A special thanks
To the people in my office—Bob, Carol, Susie, Debora, and Nancy—whose hard work and tireless assistance were invaluable in helping me write this book.
Jack Tiano

Cover photo by Gordon Smith
Photographed at Harper's Restaurant, Darien, Connecticut
Book design by Liney Li
Edited by Jay Hyams and Sharyn Perlman

First printing in 1981. Reprinted in 1990.

This edition reprinted in 1992 by SMITHMARK Publishers Inc., 16 East 32nd Street, New York, NY 10016.

SMITHMARK books are available for bulk purchase for sales promotion and premium use. For details write or call the manager of special sales, SMITHMARK Publishers Inc., 16 East 32nd Street, New York, NY 10016; (212) 532-6600.

Library of Congress Cataloging-in-Publication Data

Tiano, Jack
  The American Bartenders School guide to drinks/by Jack Tiano.
      p.   cm.
  Originally published: New York; Rutledge Press, 1981.
  Includes index.
  ISBN 0-8317-0275-3
  1. Alcoholic beverages.   2. Cocktails.   I. American Bartenders School.   II. Title
TX951.T5   1992
641.8'74—dc20   92-19393
                                                            CIP

Printed in the United States of America

Contents

INTRODUCTION

In *The American Bartenders School Guide to Drinks* we have attempted to show you the hows and whys of mixing drinks. Since 1969 we have trained thousands of men and women in the art of mixology.

Students of our schools are always amazed at how readily they master all types of basic and fancy drinks. Our students have ranged from college professors with Ph.Ds to immigrants who could barely read and write English. All of these people had one thing in common—they all found our method of learning easy and enjoyable.

We have often been asked what our secret is—how can we take all these people from diverse educational backgrounds and learning abilities and teach them in two weeks to be expert mixologists? The secret is in the method of instruction. In preparing this book, my staff and I have incorporated many of our school's techniques that have helped us in training our students. In teaching, we not only give the drink recipe, we also discuss each step of how each drink is prepared and explain the reasons for the prescribed steps.

Our bar book is not just a collection of hundreds of recipes arranged alphabetically or by liquor base. Our drink recipes are listed by method of preparation and ingredient base.

If you were to search through all the thousands of drink recipes, you would find that they can all be broken down into eight categories, or drink types. There are only eight basic drinks, and every drink ever invented is merely a simple variation of one of the eight. Once you learn the eight categories and understand the differences among them, making variations can be simple and fun.

In *The American Bartenders School Guide to Drinks*, we have broken down the most popular modern drinks, plus many old reliable standards, into the eight drink categories. In the back of the book we have cross-indexed these drinks in alphabetical order for easy reference.

Our purpose is to give you in-depth knowledge of the wonderful art of mixology. After reading this book and following the instructions, you will not only know how to make hundreds of fantastic drinks, but you will also be able to invent hundreds of your own specialties that will be quite unique.

We had lots of fun preparing this book, and we hope you will have as much fun learning many of the secrets of professional bartending.

1 THE AMERICAN BARTENDERS SCHOOL

I started the American Bartenders School in downtown Chicago in 1969. I had been a bartender for several years, and many people asked how I got into bartending. As a matter of fact, a friend of mine got me started. He was a part-time bartender in a large union hall in Chicago, which held ethnic dances with hundreds of thirsty customers. He asked me if I wanted to work with him, and, being adventurous, I agreed.

My introduction to bartending was hardly a friendly one. On my first night, I worked a Mexican dance, and most of the customers could not speak English. Adding to the trauma were a hot, humid July Chicago night and broken air conditioning. There I was, with thirteen other bartenders, facing eight hundred hot, thirsty people, dancing furiously to Latin music. Within the first ten minutes, the bar was bombarded by hundreds of people screaming in Spanish for liquid refreshments. It was like Custer's Last Stand. For eight straight hours I poured drink after drink for this unique gathering of people. It was hard, demanding work. I never stopped. It did not matter how fast I could make the drinks, because for every person I served, there were hundreds behind him, pushing their way to the bar. And those people were not ordering one drink, but several, for their friends at the tables.

I was hooked on bartending, even after that first night. I had the opportunity to come in contact with all types of people with many different traits and personalities. The fast pace and the challenge excited me. I decided to be a bartender on that hot July night.

The drinks we served at the union hall are known as basics—7&7s, Scotch and waters, beers, etc. To them a

Screwdriver was a fancy drink. I realized my knowledge of mixology was almost zero, and to work in a nice establishment, I would have to learn more.

At this point, I was in a quandary. How was I going to learn all of the facets of bartending? My mind was working overtime, trying to solve my dilemma. I had at least four plans kicking around, all of which were futile.

My first strategic maneuver was to try to get a job in a nice place and learn by apprenticeship. To my disheartenment, every place wanted experienced bartenders and wasn't interested in training anybody.

Next, I wanted to find bartenders who would train me. Each bartender who taught me had his own way of doing things. As a result, I learned little to nothing and was left totally confused.

Then the answer seemed so simple. I bought a recipe book and tried to commit hundreds of drinks to memory. That was virtually impossible. Since none of the drinks had anything in common, it was like learning calculus.

My last resort was to just plunge my way into a place and learn by doing. After making thirty phone calls to catering halls, asking if they could use a professional behind the bar, one gruff-sounding individual told me to come in for an interview.

I walked into the plush office to meet the manager, who bore a striking resemblance, in every way, to Don Corleone in *The Godfather*. The combination of the office and its occupant was overwhelming. He said he needed a professional who could make fancy drinks. I assured him I could. Little did he know the truth.

My first night there was very similar to the one at the union hall in that there were hundreds of people. However, it was a little more fancy, being a dinner for the International Travel Club. Another major discomforting difference was that people were requesting fancy drinks. I had been informed that this would occur, but I tried to push the reality that it would actually happen out of my mind. After the panic wore off, and my mind could think, I simply asked the other bartenders to make the fancy drinks for me. We were a team, and I pretended to be too busy and asked them for help when they weren't busy. They were glad to do it; if they only knew my ulterior motive. So the bird got kicked out of its nest and learned to fly.

I decided that prospective bartenders should not have to go through what I had to endure to learn the trade. That single thought led to the birth of the American Bartenders School.

After several years of actual bartending experience and much planning, I opened my first school in Chicago. As with most new ventures, it was much harder to get going than I had thought it would be. The first year I had to work as a bartender while the school became known. It was worth the hard work and sacrifice because since 1969 I have opened thirty-five schools across the nation.

Our schools are set up like no other schools. We don't have desks and blackboards. We do, however, have a bar and all the working equipment associated with a bar. Everyone who visits our schools for the first time thinks when they first walk in that they have stumbled upon an unknown cocktail lounge.

Students who attend the American and Professional Bartenders School learn all aspects of professional bartending. During their training, they practice making over 150 drinks, and we estimate that they make over 5,000 drinks during the two-week course. Each ingredient of the drink recipe has to be carefully measured, much like a pharmacist preparing prescriptions. Students learn and remember the drinks by constantly making them over and over again. It is similar to learning how to drive a car—the more a person does it, the easier it becomes until it is almost automatic.

During the two-week training period, students learn how to give courteous and efficient service. They are broken up into teams, one person being the bartender, the other the customer, and practice making and serving the drinks. We have simulated a cocktail lounge environment to make the learning as close as possible to on-the-job training. A common question is what do we do with all the drinks. The secret is that we don't use real liquor. The liquor has been carefully simulated through the use of scientifically prepared color dyes to resemble and mix like real liquor.

We give lectures on how to handle various situations that occur with customers. Students also receive lectures on alcoholic beverages—how they are made and their differences. It is the school's philosophy that there is much more to being a professional bartender than just knowing a few drink recipes.

Since I opened the first school, we have trained over 50,000 men and women of all ages to be professional bartenders. We have graduates working in all fifty states and seventy-six foreign countries. Our school's job placement service has placed our graduates in over 35,000 establishments.

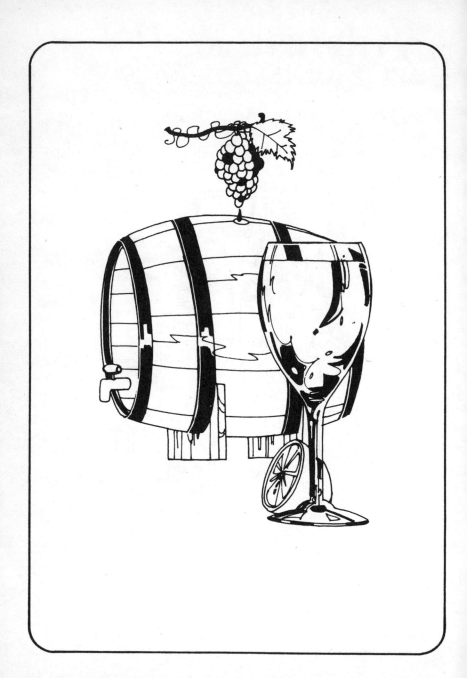

2 THE HISTORY OF MIXED DRINKS

The exact date of the first mixed drink is a matter of pure speculation and great conjecture. However, it was probably a few minutes after wine was discovered. The farmer probably did not like the taste of the fermented grapes and mixed the wine with water or possibly squeezed in the juice of a local fruit to change the harsh taste.

Since that early dawning of man's inventive nature, we have had a long history of mixologists who either enjoyed the effect of alcoholic beverages but did not particularly like their tastes, or who just wanted something different.

In my years of bartending, I have found that things have changed. People who drink alcoholic beverages can be broken down into two groups: people who like the distinct flavor of alcoholic beverages, and those who prefer to disguise it with a variety of mixes. The first group of people probably order martinis, liquor on the rocks, or liquor with a non-flavored mix such as water or soda. The second group order fancy mixed drinks, such as a Tom Collins or a Whisky Sour. Neither group is superior or more sophisticated than the other—it is just a matter of personal taste.

In the early 1900s, bartenders poured mostly beer and whisky. People usually had their whisky straight, and on occasion, to double the effect, would mix it with the beer. With their limited supply of alcoholic beverages, this was the most popular mixed drink.

Rum was popular in the 1600s and early 1700s, and there are a few recipes from that period. In the late 1800s and early 1900s, mixed drinks slowly became more popular. This resulted from women coming out of the kitchen and dining out more often. On occasion, indulgence in spirits, although frowned upon, was acceptable. Since it would be shocking for a woman to have a straight whisky or beer, liquor was mixed with another liquid to dilute it and make it more agreeable. The first mixes used were cream, citrus juices where available, and, later, soft drinks.

Mixed drinks did not really gain wide acceptance or popularity until Prohibition in 1922. The age of bathtub gin and bootleg whisky really started it all. Many times the illegal liquor was so coarse and poor tasting that it had to be mixed with heavily flavored liquids to make it drinkable. Drinks like Whisky Sours, Pink Ladys, Tom Collins, and Alexanders, were introduced to the masses of illegal drinkers. The habit of mixing liquors with Coca Cola, 7Up, and other soft drinks became popular.

At the end of Prohibition, there was a whole new style of drinking. There were still many who preferred their liquor straight, with a glass of beer on the side, but there were also many who liked their drinks mixed with lemon juice, cream, or soft drinks. The age of the cocktail was upon us.

In the 1940s, women became even more emancipated—working in war plants, while raising a family. It became more acceptable for women to have a drink, but without the harshness. Thus the 7&7, Rum and Coke, Daiquiri, and Bacardi became popular.

The 1950s brought the era of a new generation of drinkers. A liquor named vodka swept the country in popularity. A Moscow Mule, made with ginger beer and vodka, was heavily advertised by Smirnoff. Soon professional and home bartenders alike were mixing vodka with every imaginable mix, creating scores of new cocktails. Screwdrivers, Bloody Marys, and Gimlets became the rage. A large group of American drinkers had developed a liking for sweets from their childhood days and carried this craving into their adult socializing. In the early 1970s, an explosion came about. Liquor distillers and importers saw an almost unknown liqueur, Galliano, zoom in sales by the promotion of a drink called the Harvey Wallbanger, which used Galliano. This sweet, creamy orange-juice flavored concoction took the nation by storm. Its catchy name made headlines in *Time* magazine. Everyone wanted to try it.

Since the Harvey Wallbanger, new drinks are being invented daily with a variety of liquors and liqueurs. Many distillers have invented new exotic-flavored liqueurs from coconuts, pineapples, melons, and many other things. With each of these new liqueurs, scads of mixtures are added to make unique and unusual tasting drinks. Most of the drinks remain popular for only a short time before new ones take their places. However, a few linger on and become standards.

In the 1940s, the average bartender knew how to prepare twenty-five mixed drinks. Today's professional mixologist knows an average of 150 mixed drinks, a 600 percent increase.

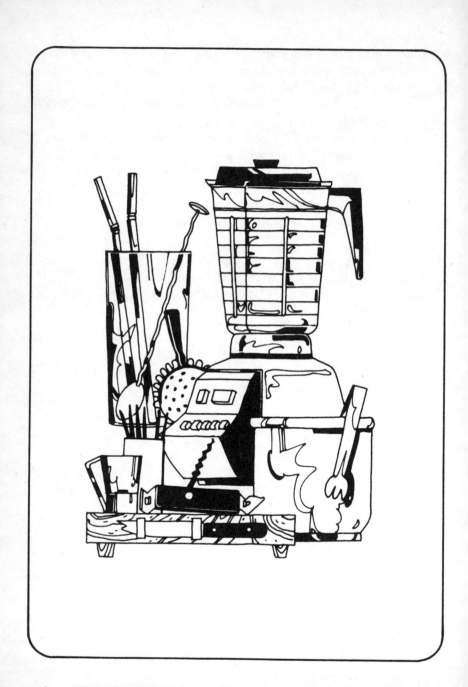

3 BAR EQUIPMENT

BAR SPOON
Used for stirring drinks that are made in a glass mixing cup, such as Martinis and Manhattans, the bar spoon measures one teaspoon.

CORKSCREW, CAN AND BOTTLE OPENERS
A corkscrew is necessary to open wine.
Have a can opener for tomato and other juices.
You need a bottle opener for beer, bottled mixes, etc.
NOTE: Usually, all three instruments can be found in one handy tool.

ELECTRIC BLENDER
The ingredients in some drinks, such as Brandy Alexanders, Margaritas, etc., need to be thoroughly blended. Blending them in an electric blender is the best method.

ICE, ICE BUCKET, TONGS, SCOOP
There are three kinds of ice: cubed, crushed, and shaved. Shaved is ice which has been crushed twice. Ice cubes (rocks) are used most often. Crushed is sometimes used to make drinks like Margaritas, to achieve the frozen effect.
To avoid running to the refrigerator every time you need ice, keep it in a bucket of some kind.
Ice tongs or a scoop should be used to handle ice. Never scoop ice with the glass you are using. You'll risk breaking the glass in the ice.

MEASURING DEVICES
Even the most professional bartender measures the ingredients of every drink, even though experience may permit

some to do this by eye and skillful freehand pouring. However, to make a perfect drink every time, measure all ingredients. Many drinks can be spoiled by being too strong or too weak.

There are several different measuring devices. It is a personal decision as to which one suits you best.

A measuring glass cup is marked like those used in cooking. Shot glasses come in varied sizes, from ¾ ounce to 1½ ounces. A stainless-steel, double-sided shot glass is convenient. One end is 1 ounce, the other is 1½ ounces, which is also called a jigger.

MIXING CUP—GLASS
Drinks such as Martinis and Manhattans are stirred in the glass mixing cup.

MIXING CUP—METAL
Drinks such as Grasshoppers and Whisky Sours are blended in the metal mixing cup, on a malt-shop type of blender. Or, the metal cup can be used in conjunction with the glass cup to shake drinks when an electric blender is not available.

PARING KNIFE AND CUTTING BOARD
A good paring knife is essential for cutting fruit, and that is all it should be used for.

A small cutting board, which can easily be kept in the bar, is very convenient for fruit cutting.

PICKS, STICKS, STRAWS, NAPKINS
Picks make the handling of garnishes a lot easier. Use picks for olives, onions, etc.

Swizzle sticks and straws are stirring devices. They go in any drink that is served over ice.

Cocktail napkins (small ones) are placed under the drink to absorb the moisture that forms on the glass due to condensation. It is a nice touch to use a napkin with all drinks, even coffee or hot drinks.

SALT AND SUGAR CONTAINERS
Have two small saucers for salt and sugar. This makes it easy to salt a Margarita glass quickly.

SPEED POURERS
Professional bartenders use speed pourers to give them control over how fast (or slow) the liquor flows from the bottle.

STRAINER
After making a blended or stirred drink, place the strainer over the mixing cup and strain the mixture into the glass. This prevents ice from being poured in the finished drink.

TOWELS
Have a moistened terry-cloth towel handy for keeping the bar area clean.

For drying glasses, use a dry cotton towel.

4 THE HOME BAR

If you have ever walked into a liquor store, you have seen hundreds of different brands and types of liquors. What type of liquor and how much to get can be a mind-boggling decision. To help you out, here are a few simple guidelines to follow.

In stocking your bar for the first time, don't attempt to buy all types of exotic liquors and liqueurs, unless you can afford it. Your liquor inventory should be based on the items you'll use the most, and that will depend on what drinks you and your friends prefer. Keep in mind that you'll save money on any liquor by buying the large size, 1¾ liters (formerly ½ gallon). Also, watch for sale items.

The list of spirits below is a reasonable guide to get you started. If there are certain liquors or liqueurs that you particularly like, you may want to double the amount.

HOME BAR LIQUORS AND LIQUEURS

Amount	Spirit	
1 bottle (1¾ liters)	vodka	Vodka, being a grain neutral spirit, has virtually no flavor. There is very little difference between the off brands and the more expensive name brands. However, if you like your vodka straight, you may prefer a premium vodka.

1 bottle (750 ml)	bourbon	Bourbon may be used in any recipe calling for American whisky (or just whisky).
1 bottle (750 ml)	Scotch	We suggest a light-flavored Scotch.
1 bottle (750 ml)	Canadian	Canadians are very smooth, and are becoming more popular in the United States.
1 bottle (1¾ liters)	gin	The flavor of gin will vary depending on the brand. We suggest a light-flavored gin.
1 bottle (1¾ liters)	rum	Although there are three types of rum, we suggest the white rum; it is the lightest tasting. If you prefer a heavy rum taste, you may want to include a bottle of dark rum.
1 bottle (1¾ liters)	tequila	The white tequila is the most popular.
1 bottle (750 ml)	brandy	The domestics are very good and much less expensive than the imported French cognacs.
generally small sizes	triple sec creme de menthe creme de cacao Kahlua amaretto Drambuie Irish Mist Benedictine Galliano	These liqueurs are nice to have alone and are also primary ingredients in popular drinks.

1 bottle (small)	dry vermouth	The taste of vermouth will vary with the distiller. Most Americans prefer a mild, light-tasting dry vermouth.
1 bottle (small)	sweet vermouth	Because of the sugar content in sweet vermouth, it will last a long time after being opened.
Approximately 2 six-packs	beer	Have regular and low-calorie light on hand.
1 bottle (1¾ liters)	white wine	Chablis is enjoyed alone or with meals.
1 bottle (1¾ liters)	burgundy wine	It's nice to have some red wine on hand, especially if you are serving beef.
1 bottle (1¾ liters)	rosé wine	Rosé is popular alone or with meals.

NON-ALCOHOLIC MIXES

Bloody Mary mix	Pre-mixed tomato juice and spices
club soda	Buy it in individual bottles; the 12-ounce size will make two drinks. If you are having a party, large bottles are more economical.

cola	The brand is a matter of personal taste
coffee	When you are using coffee for hot drinks, always make it fresh and make sure it is steaming hot.
cream	If you don't use it in your daily coffee, keep cream frozen until you intend to use it. When preparing drinks, always keep it chilled.
ginger ale	Buy it in individual bottles, the 12-ounce size
grapefruit juice	A must if you like a Salty Dog or Greyhound
grenadine	A sweet, cherry colored syrup, made from the pulp of pomegranates. It can be stored indefinitely without spoiling.
lemon juice	Use sweet and sour for recipes calling for lemon juice. It is convenient and has a long storage life.
lime juice	Rose's is the best known, but in recent years, many new brands have come on the market. It is a tart, sweetened lime syrup, rather than a substitute for fresh lime juice.
orange juice	A Screwdriver is a very popular drink, and many people are now mixing a variety of liquors with orange juice.
Orange Flower Water	If you like Ramos Fizzes, you should have this.

orgeat	An almond syrup, used in Mai Tais and other tropical drinks
passion fruit juice or nectar	Tropical juices, used in rum drinks
Pina Colada mix	Pre-mixed pineapple and cream of coconut syrup.
pineapple juice	Buy small cans—large if you are having a party. To store canned juices after opening, pour in glass or plastic container and cover tightly.
quinine water	The same as tonic, buy in individual small bottles
seltzer water	The same as club soda
7Up	It is the most popular of all the lemon-lime soft drinks
sweet and sour	This is marketed under a variety of names, from Daiquiri mix to Margarita mix, etc. It is reconstituted lemon juice, with sugar and bar foam added. Keep several quarts on hand.
tomato juice	Straight tomato juice is richer than tomato cocktail. Jars rather than cans are best for storage in the refrigerator once opened.
tonic	The same as quinine
water	Bottled spring water is the most desirable—it has no chlorine or harsh-tasting minerals.

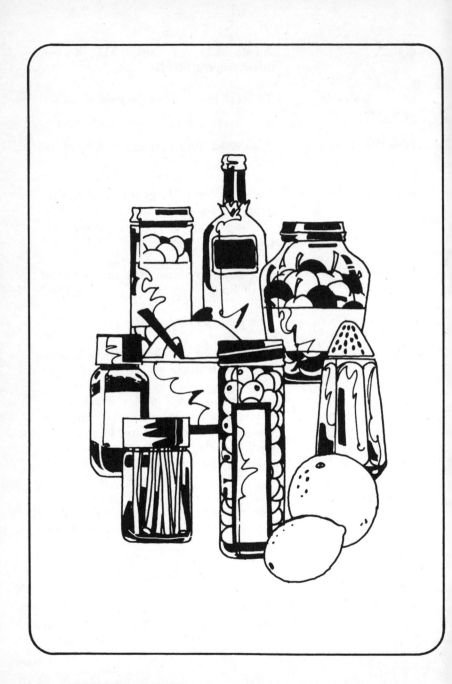

5 ODDS AND ENDS

These are the basic extras you should have on hand to complete your home bar inventory.

bitters
: The best known is Angostura. It is flavored with roots, barks, and herbs, and has a unique bitterness. It once was a vital part of the Manhattan recipe and is still used in an Old Fashioned.

cherries
: Use the maraschino, a popular garnish for Manhattans, Sours, and tropical drinks.

cinnamon sticks
: Buy the extra-long kind, used to stir and add flavoring in many of the hot, non-coffee drinks

lemons
: The rinds are used for lemon twists which are becoming a popular garnish for Martinis and other drinks

limes
: Cut into quarters for lime squeezes to be used in a variety of drinks

nutmeg
: Sprinkle on Alexanders, or use as a topping on many hot, non-coffee drinks

olives
: They come in many types and sizes. The small, green pitted ones are the most popular, but you can get them stuffed with pimentos, anchovies, onions, or almonds. Keep them refrigerated and tightly closed.

onions	A popular garnish for those Martini drinkers who like something different. A Martini with a pearled onion is called a Gibson.
oranges	When sliced, they provide a colorful garnish for sours and tropical drinks
salt	A must for a Margarita or a "scratch" Bloody Mary
sugar	Use the super-fine grade; it dissolves easily

BOTTLE SIZES AND STANDARD BAR MEASUREMENTS

As of December 31, 1979, all liquor bottles were converted to the metric system.

Spirits

old size names	old size fluid oz.	new metric sizes fluid oz.	new metr. sizes
miniature	1.6	1.7	50 ml.
½ pint	8.	6.8	200 ml.
pint	16.	16.9	500 ml.
fifth	25.6	25.4	750 ml.
quart	32.	33.8	1 liter
½ gallon	64.	59.2	1.75 liter

Wines

old size names	old size fluid oz.	new metric sizes fluid oz.	new metric sizes
miniature	2, 3, or 4	3.4	100 ml.
2/5 pint	6.4	6.3	187 ml.
4/5 pint	12.8	12.7	375 ml.
fifth	25.6	25.4	750 ml.
quart	32.	33.8	1 liter
2/5 gallon	51.2	50.7	1.5 liters
4/5 gallon	102.4	101.4	3 liters

STANDARD BAR MEASUREMENTS

1 teaspoon (bar spoon)	⅛ ounce
1 tablespoon	⅜ ounce
1 pony	1 ounce
1 jigger	1½ ounces
1 wineglass	4 ounces
1 split	6 ounces
1 cup	8 ounces

6 TECHNIQUES

GLASSWARE

All the recipes in this book indicate the type of glass you can use with each drink. In the last several years, there has been a trend toward using multipurpose glassware—the advantage is that you can avoid having a lot of different styles of glasses, some of which you may use only occasionally. You can get by with as few as four different styles, and they will easily accommodate every drink recipe. Pictured at the beginning of each drink category are several different styles of glasses you can use. The style you choose will really be a matter of personal taste.

No matter what style of glass you choose, there are a few basic rules you should follow. Always keep your glassware sparkling clean. Keep one towel handy for drying and one for polishing. Always use a stemmed glass for cocktails served without ice, so that the heat of your hand will not warm the drink. If you are using oversized stemmed wine glasses, don't worry if the recipe doesn't fill the glass totally. Always serve drinks with cocktail napkins or coasters to absorb the moisture of the outside of the glass. If this is not done, condensation will form at the bottom of the glass and leave a water ring.

CHILLING GLASSWARE

Stemmed glassware should be well chilled to keep the drinks cold. The easiest way is to refrigerate them at least one hour in advance. If you don't have time, fill each glass with cracked, shaved, or crushed ice, before mixing the drink. When the drink is ready, empty the ice out of the glass, wipe the outside of the glass with a dry towel, and pour the drink.

FROSTING GLASSWARE

There are two methods of frosting glassware. To frost beer mugs or cocktail glasses, dip them in water and place them in the freezer for thirty minutes. The glass will come out with a white, frosted, ice-cold look and feel. Frosting beer mugs will make the beer very cold, but it will also remove some of the beer's flavor.

If you are frosting glassware with salt to make a Margarita, moisten the rim of a pre-chilled glass with a slice of lime or lemon, then dip the rim into salt. This same method is used for frosting a glass with sugar.

STIRRING DRINKS

When you are making drinks containing liquors of different densities, and when cream or sweet and sour is not involved, the drinks should be stirred rather than blended. Be sure to stir liquor-and-mix drinks gently to preserve the sparkle and effervescence of the mix used.

BLENDING OR SHAKING

Drinks using ingredients that don't mix easily, like cream, sweet and sour, or eggs, should be blended in an electric blender or shaken by hand.

POURING

If you are making multiples of the same cocktail, make the drinks in one batch. Generally, you can make up to four cocktails in an electric blender or shaking cup. To insure equal portions in each glass, set up the required number of glasses in a row. Pour, filling each glass only halfway. Then go back to the first glass and finish.

HOW TO FLOAT LIQUEURS
Different liquors or liqueurs will float on top of each other depending on their density and thickness. The easiest way to do this, if you have the time, is to pour the liqueurs into the glass and place the glass in the refrigerator. Within an hour, each liqueur will find its own weight level, forming distinct layers. If you don't have the time, hold a bar spoon upside down, above the glass, and pour the liqueur over the back part of the spoon. Do this slowly. The spoon breaks the fall of the fluid, and will allow it to gently settle on top of the other liqueur(s).

HOW TO FLAME LIQUOR
Setting liquor or liqueurs on fire can be dangerous. Flaming drinks look pretty, but if you are not careful, you could set someone or something on fire. If you decide to flame liquors, make certain that the glass, cooking vessel, and liquor are all pre-warmed. Start with a teaspoon or tablespoon of liquor, preheat over the flame, then set afire. Pour flaming liquid carefully into the remaining liquor to be set afire.

7 PARTY ENTERTAINING

No matter what type of party you're having—cocktail, Sunday brunch, outdoor cookout, or holiday bash—the amount and type of liquor you should have on hand will depend on several factors. For an average party that will last four hours, you should plan on each guest consuming three or four drinks. If you plan on having a longer party, each guest will probably consume one to two drinks each additional hour. You should also take into consideration any special drinking preferences of your guests. If you know they especially like Martinis, Black Russians, or white wine, plan your liquor purchases around what you are sure they'll enjoy. The other thing to understand is that your guests won't expect you to serve or have the spirits to make hundreds of different drinks. In fact, the larger the guest list, the more you'll probably want to limit the choice of drinks.

There are certain basic liquors and mixes you should have available for every type of party. Your guests may or may not drink everything you have available, but I have always found it better to have a little too much than not enough. The things you purchase for your party won't spoil and will last indefinitely. If you don't use it all, you'll have extra to enjoy later.

Here is a basic list of liquors, mixes, and supplies you should have on hand for a party of twenty guests. If your party has more or fewer people, simply adjust your buying accordingly. To be on the safe side, always figure on having 20 percent more guests than invited. Without fail someone always brings along a friend that just happened to pop in unexpectedly.

GLASSWARE

Glassware always seems to run out mid-way through the party no matter how much you have. You should figure a minimum of two glasses for each guest. Don't worry about having a large variety, generally a highball and a rock style will be sufficient in which to serve your drinks. If you're having an exceptionally large party, you may want to consider renting glassware from a party rental service.

ICE

There never seems to be enough ice. Your home refrigerator won't be able to handle it, so plan on buying extra ice. You should have at least two pounds for every guest.

CANAPES

Drinking stimulates hunger. Having something for your guests to munch on will make your party better. Stay away from chicken salad, tuna fish salad, and other such combinations. They quickly become warm and soggy and your guests probably won't eat them. After a number of drinks, guests get tired of tidbits. If you wish them to stay, plan on serving something of substance like ham or chicken. Avoid serving candy as sugar does not mix with alcohol.

BEVERAGE SUPPLIES

The type and amount of liquor you should have on hand will vary with the type and time of your party. Daytime or early evening parties generally require less liquor than evening parties. You should count on each 750 ml. bottle to contain approximately twenty drinks. This is based on 1 ounce to 1½ ounces per drink with spillage. If you have any control over the pouring of the liquor, you should not allow the drinks to be any stronger or your guests will quickly get "zonked." Remember that too much liquor in a drink can spoil it by making it too strong. To avoid overpouring by your guests, either hire a bartender and instruct him how much to pour, or leave several shot glasses or jiggers by the liquor bottles. Hopefully, your guests will get the hint and use them to measure their liquor if you're allowing them to do their own pouring.

BASIC PARTY SUPPLY LIST

amount	size	liquor
1	750 ml.	Scotch
1	750 ml.	American whisky
1	750 ml.	tequila
1	750 ml.	gin
2	750 ml.	vodka
1	750 ml.	light rum
2	1.5 ml.	chablis wine
2	1.5 ml.	burgundy wine
2	1.5 ml.	rosé wine
1	small	dry vermouth
1	small	sweet vermouth
1	case	beer
3	750 ml.	liqueurs: Kahlua, amaretto, Galliano, or whatever your personal preference.

amount	size	mix
6	quarts	club soda
6	quarts	tonic
4	quarts	cola
4	quarts	7Up
3	quarts	orange juice
3	quarts	tomato juice
4	quarts	sweet & sour
1	bottle	lime juice
4	quarts	water

fruits and fixings

olives
lemon twists
lime squeezes
maraschino cherries
cocktail napkins
swizzle sticks/straws

You may want to add certain types of liquor and increase your amounts of mixes if you are having a specialty type party.

BRUNCH
You want to serve Bloody Marys, Screwdrivers, Salty Dogs, Greyhounds, Ramos Fizzes, or Mimosas. They are great early afternoon drinks.

COCKTAIL
Martinis, Manhattans, and liquor-and-mix drinks are very popular. You may also want to make up a few specialty drinks in advance, like Strawberry Margaritas or Daiquiris. Pre-mix all the ingredients in advance and have them in pitchers next to your electric blender.

DINNER
You should have a white or red wine to go with dinner. Figure on two to three glasses per guest. For dessert, have a cream drink made with ice cream, some specialty coffee drinks, straight brandy, or float liqueurs to make Pousse Cafes.

COOKOUT
You want to serve summer drinks like short or long sours. You should also have lots of beer, wine, and soft drinks on hand.

HOLIDAY

If you live in a cold climate, have some hot drinks available, or a special type punch. Fruit-flavored brandies are very popular when the snow hits the ground.

PUNCHES

Punches fit right in with certain kinds of parties, especially holiday gatherings. A special champagne punch on New Year's Eve is a must. Christmas Eve wouldn't be the same without an eggnog punch. Punches seem to complement birthday parties or special celebrations. It would not be appropriate, however, to serve a punch at a cocktail or dinner party. People at those functions usually stick with mixed drinks.

Punches are economical both in time and money. Once your punch is made and served, you don't have to worry about people not having a drink, they just help themselves. Since a lot of punches contain mostly juices, you'll save money on liquor. Non-alcoholic punches are great for children or non-drinkers. It saves you from having to buy individual cans of soda, etc.

8 CREAM DRINKS

HIGHLIGHTS

Cream drinks are very sweet, smooth, and pleasing to the palate. These drinks are great for anyone who has a sweet tooth. They are perfect after-dinner drinks, and many people like to serve them instead of dessert. For those people who prefer mild-tasting cocktails, cream drinks are ideal because they don't have a strong alcoholic taste.

All cream drinks use coffee cream as a base ingredient and liqueurs for flavoring. Liqueurs were discovered by medieval monks in Europe for medical purposes. In the Middle Ages, liqueurs were the principle antiseptics for dressing wounds as well as remedies for many diseases. The monks grew all types of plants, roots, and herbs (many of which are still being used in modern medicine), and mixed them with crude alcoholic spirits. Sweet syrups were gradually added to make the mixtures more palatable. Today's liqueurs are made from a wide variety of fruits, roots, plants, seeds, and herbs. Some liqueurs use over twenty different ingredients. Liqueurs have a sweet syrupy flavor and must have a minimum of 2.5 percent sugar by volume. Each liqueur has a distinct flavor because of the special mixture of ingredients.

You will find that the taste of each cream drink will greatly resemble the unique flavor of the liqueurs you use. It is quite easy to invent your own cream drink recipes by combining your favorite liqueurs with the cream base. In the chapter Liqueur Reference, you will find a list of liqueurs, with a brief description of their flavors. Pick out the ones that appeal to you, experiment with them, and have fun. Who knows—maybe you'll invent a recipe that will sweep the nation and make you famous. It has happened before.

While you're experimenting, try this interesting variation of the preparation of cream drinks. Use a scoop of vanilla ice cream in place of the coffee cream. It will taste like a flavored milk shake with an alcoholic kick.

METHODS OF PREPARING CREAM DRINKS

There are two ways to prepare cream drinks—you can either mix them in an electric blender or you can shake them by hand. I prefer using a blender because it thoroughly mixes the ingredients together and gives the drink a creamy, frothy flavor. Some old-time bartenders on the East coast prefer the old-fashioned way of shaking the ingredients by hand in a cocktail shaking set. I personally don't like cream drinks shaken by hand, because the cream and the heavy, sweet liqueurs don't mix thoroughly enough. The drink comes out tasting flat, like flavored milk.

GLASSWARE

The types of glasses used for cream drinks vary with personal preference. The most important thing to remember, though, is that a stemmed glass with a minimum capacity of five ounces will always be used. If you choose a large wine goblet (stemmed), don't be concerned that the drink won't fill the glass entirely. After being blended, the drink will only fill four to five ounces of any glass. It is perfectly acceptable to serve these drinks with the glass only half filled.

Cream drinks are chilled to a maximum degree of coldness in the mixing cup while being blended. When the drink is strained into the glass, it will not contain any ice. The drink will only become warmer as time passes. The glass will be pre-chilled either by icing it or by placing it in the freezer. Even though the glass is chilled, you are still pouring a cold drink into a "warm" glass. Always handle the glass by the stem to prevent the heat of your hand from transferring to the part of the glass containing the drink.

Below are examples of popular stemmed glasses you may want to include in your home bar inventory.

CHAMPAGNE

COCKTAIL

COCKTAIL

PREPARATION FOR CREAM DRINKS

1 Chill stemmed glass by filling it with ice.

2 Fill ¼ blending cup with ice.

3 Measure liqueurs first. Add cream.

4 Blend at medium speed for 5 seconds.
If shaking, shake at least 12 times.

5 Remove ice from chilled glass.

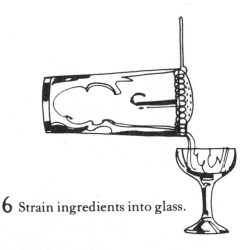

6 Strain ingredients into glass.

Alexander

Stemmed glass, chilled
Mixing cup, ¼ filled with ice
½ oz. gin
½ oz. white creme de cacao
2 oz. cream
Blend and strain
Nutmeg garnish

Almond Joy

Stemmed glass, chilled
Mixing cup, ¼ filled with ice
½ oz. amaretto
½ oz. white creme de cacao
2 oz. cream
Blend and strain

Banshee

Stemmed glass, chilled
Mixing cup, ¼ filled with ice
½ oz. white creme de cacao
½ oz. creme de banana
2 oz. cream
Blend and strain

Blue Carnation

Stemmed glass, chilled
Mixing cup, ¼ filled with ice
½ oz. white creme de cacao
½ oz. blue curacao
2 oz. cream
Blend and strain

Brandy Alexander

Stemmed glass, chilled
Mixing cup, ¼ filled with ice
½ oz. brandy
½ oz. brown creme de cacao
2 oz. cream
Blend and strain
Nutmeg garnish

Brown Bomber

Stemmed glass, chilled
Mixing cup, ¼ filled with ice
½ oz. peanut liqueur
½ oz. white creme de cacao
2 oz. cream
Blend and strain

Climax

Stemmed glass, chilled
Mixing cup, ¼ filled with ice
½ oz. white creme de cacao
½ oz. amaretto
½ oz. triple sec
½ oz. vodka
½ oz. creme de banana
1 oz. cream
Blend and strain

Creamsickle

Stemmed glass, chilled
Mixing cup, ¼ filled with ice
½ oz. vodka
½ oz. triple sec
½ oz. orange juice
1½ oz. cream
Blend and strain

Dutch Velvet

Stemmed glass, chilled
Mixing cup, ¼ filled with ice
½ oz. chocolate mint liqueur
½ oz. banana liqueur
2 oz. cream
Blend and strain
Garnish with 1 teaspoon
    shaved sweet chocolate

Foxy Lady

Stemmed glass, chilled
Mixing cup, ¼ filled with ice
½ oz. amaretto
½ oz. brown creme de cacao
2 oz. cream
Blend and strain

Golden Cadillac

Stemmed glass, chilled
Mixing cup, ¼ filled with ice
½ oz. white creme de cacao
½ oz. Galliano
2 oz. cream
Blend and strain

Golden Dream

Stemmed glass, chilled
Mixing cup, ¼ filled with ice
½ oz. Galliano
½ oz. triple sec
½ oz. orange juice
1½ oz. cream
Blend and strain

Grasshopper

Stemmed glass, chilled
Mixing cup, ¼ filled with ice
½ oz. white creme de cacao
½ oz. green creme de menthe
2 oz. cream
Blend and strain

Italian Delight

Stemmed glass, chilled
Mixing cup, ¼ filled with ice
1 oz. amaretto
½ oz. orange juice
1½ oz. cream
Blend and strain
Cherry garnish

Orgasm

Stemmed glass, chilled
Mixing cup, ¼ filled with ice
½ oz. white creme de cacao
½ oz. amaretto
½ oz. triple sec
½ oz. vodka
1 oz. cream
Blend and strain

Pineapple Francine

Stemmed glass, chilled
Mixing cup, ¼ filled with ice
½ oz. rum
½ oz. apricot brandy
1 oz. pineapple juice
1 oz. cream
1 oz. canned crushed
    pineapple
Blend and strain

Pink Lady

Stemmed glass, chilled
Mixing cup, ¼ filled with ice
1 oz. gin
½ oz. grenadine
1½ oz. cream
Blend and strain

Pink Squirrel

Stemmed glass, chilled
Mixing cup, ¼ filled with ice
½ oz. white creme de cacao
½ oz. creme de almond or,
    creme de noyaux
2 oz. cream
Blend and strain

Screaming Banana Banshee

Stemmed glass, chilled
Mixing cup, ¼ filled with ice
½ oz. banana liqueur
½ oz. vodka
½ oz. white creme de cacao
1½ oz. cream
Blend and strain
Cherry garnish

Strawberry Banana Split

Large stemmed glass, chilled
Mixing cup, ¼ filled with ice
1 oz. banana liqueur
½ oz. dark rum
4 oz. frozen strawberries,
    thawed
1½ oz. cream
1 teaspoon vanilla extract
½ banana, peeled and cut into
    slices (save one slice of
    banana)
Blend and strain
Garnish with whipped cream,
    1 banana slice, and 1 whole
    strawberry

Toasted Almond

Stemmed glass, chilled
Mixing cup, ¼ filled with ice
½ oz. Kahlua
½ oz. amaretto
2 oz. cream
Blend and strain

Velvet Hammer

Stemmed glass, chilled
Mixing cup, ¼ filled with ice
½ oz. white creme de cacao
½ oz. triple sec
2 oz. cream
Blend and strain

White Elephant
White Lady

Stemmed glass, chilled
Mixing cup, ¼ filled with ice
½ oz. vodka
½ oz. white creme de cacao
2 oz. cream
Blend and strain

White Heart

Stemmed glass, chilled
Mixing cup, ¼ filled with ice
½ oz. sambuca
½ oz. white creme de cacao
2 oz. cream
Blend and strain

ICE-CREAM TREATS

As mentioned previously, ice cream may be substituted for cream. Below are many special dessert drinks using ice cream. When you experiment with ice-cream drinks, you may want to try using fresh or canned fruit along with your favorite liqueurs. You can also top any of these drinks with whipped cream, as desired.

To make ice-cream drinks thicker, put ¼ cup of crushed ice in the blender but do not strain when pouring.

Banana Tree

Large stemmed glass, chilled
Mixing cup
1 oz. creme de banana
½ oz. white creme de cacao
½ oz. Galliano
½ banana, sliced and peeled
5 oz. vanilla ice cream
4 drops vanilla extract
Blend and pour
Garnish with 1 banana slice
    with skin, dipped in 2 oz.
    pineapple juice

Caramel Nut

Large stemmed glass, chilled
Mixing cup
1 oz. creme de cacao
1 oz. caramel liqueur
5 oz. soft vanilla ice cream
Blend and pour
Garnish with whipped cream
    and chopped nuts

Chocolate Black Russian

Large stemmed glass, chilled
Mixing cup
1 oz. Kahlua
½ oz. vodka
5 oz. chocolate ice cream
Blend and pour

Chocolate Snow Bear

Large stemmed glass, chilled
Mixing cup
1 oz. amaretto
1 oz. creme de cacao
5 oz. French vanilla ice cream
¼ oz. chocolate syrup
2 dashes vanilla extract
Blend and pour

Chocolatier

Large stemmed glass, chilled
Mixing cup
1 oz. light rum
1 oz. creme de cacao
5 oz. chocolate ice cream
Blend and pour
Garnish with 1 tbs. sweet
    chocolate shavings

Coconut Toastie

Stemmed glass, chilled
Mixing cup
1 oz. light rum
5 tbs. vanilla ice cream
¼ oz. whipping cream
Blend and pour
Garnish with toasted
    shredded coconut

Emerald Isle Cooler

Tall, 14-oz. glass, chilled
Place in glass:
5 oz. vanilla ice cream
Add:
1 oz. creme de menthe
1 oz. Irish whisky
Stir well
Fill glass with chilled club
    soda
Stir again

Hummer

Large stemmed glass, chilled
Mixing cup
1 oz. coffee liqueur
1 oz. light rum
5 oz. vanilla ice cream
Blend and pour
Garnish with 1 tsp. sweet or
    bittersweet chocolate,
    shaved

Pistachio Cream

Large stemmed glass, chilled
Mixing cup
1 oz. pistachio liqueur
1 oz. brandy
5 oz. vanilla ice cream
Blend and pour

Silver Cloud

Large stemmed glass, chilled
Mixing cup
½ oz. amaretto
½ oz. white creme de cacao
5 oz. soft vanilla ice cream or,
    1½ oz. whipping cream
Blend and pour
Garnish by drizzling ½ oz.
    coffee liqueur over
    whipped cream

9 SOURS

HIGHLIGHTS

Sours can be broken down into two categories—short sours and long sours. Short sours are composed of a liquor and sweetened lemon or lime juice. Long sours have the same ingredients with the addition of soda water to cut the sour taste. Also, long sours are garnished with cherries and are served in tall glasses.

The base ingredient in all sours is lemon or lime juice, with sugar added to offset the tart taste. Fresh juices were once used, but are now a rarity. Old recipe books call for the juice of one lemon or lime and one bar spoon (teaspoon) of sugar. This was the pioneering stage of what is now generally known as sweet and sour mix, or sometimes Whisky Sour mix, Daiquiri mix, etc. There are many brands of commercial sweet and sour pre-mixes, which are all quite good. They are very convenient because the lemons are squeezed for you and the sugar is already added. They also add a product called Bar Foam, which gives a drink a frothy, creamy head. Sweet and sour will keep for a long time because of its added preservatives, so it doesn't have to be refrigerated. Pre-mixes are relatively inexpensive, too. A quart, which makes from twelve to fourteen drinks, will cost about one dollar. Using fresh lemons or limes, plus the sugar, would cost three to four times as much. Using fresh fruits would also depend on which fruits were available at that time of the year, and whether or not the crops were plentiful.

If you have the time and don't mind the extra expense, you may want to make your own sour mix, using fresh lemons or limes. It will probably taste better than a pre-mix,

Recipe for Sour Mix

12 oz. lemon juice (or 6
  lemons)
18 oz. distilled or purified
  water
¼ cup refined sugar
1 egg white (small or medium
  egg)
Blend in a blender or shake in
  a quart jar
Always blend or shake before
  use, as ingredients tend to
  settle.
It will keep from 7 to 10 days.
  No more.
REFRIGERATED
ONLY.

but it is a lot of work, and it must be refrigerated or it will spoil within a week.

When the old recipes called for lime juice instead of lemon juice, it was because limes were more available in the area where the drink was invented. For example, there is an abundance of limes in Cuba and Mexico, where the Daiquiri and Margarita originated, respectively. Lemon juice is slightly more tart than lime juice, but they both achieve the same purpose—adding tartness to the drink. Pre-mixes primarily use lemon juice.

Sours can be made with any liquor. We have given you the most popular recipes. Once again, experiment with your favorite spirits, and you'll be surprised at how many variations you'll enjoy.

Several of the sour drinks have colorful histories.

The Bacardi Cocktail was invented by the Bacardi Rum

Company. The Bacardi Company is the largest rum manufacturer in the world. There are many imitations, but no rum can compare with Bacardi's consistently high quality. It was Bacardi's contention that a Bacardi Cocktail served in commercial establishments would not be a true Bacardi if it was made with any other brand of rum. In 1936, they took a lawsuit to the Supreme Court of New York because a hotel was using another rum in its Bacardi Cocktails. They won the case, and to this day it is still a legal misrepresentation to use a rum other than Bacardi in a Bacardi Cocktail.

The Daiquiri was named after the copper mines near Santiago, Cuba. An American engineer, Jennings Cox, decided to treat some visiting V.I.P.s to a special drink. He squeezed the juice from the fresh limes that were growing by his house, added some sugar, and, for the final zest, the local rum. It made such an impression on his guests that during the course of their travels, when ordering cocktails, they requested the drink they had by the Daiquiri mines.

The Collins originated in jolly old England during the 1800s. It was named after a waiter, John Collins, who was working at the Limmer's Hotel in London. Most of his customers drank gin and soda. On a hot summer day, John decided to enhance their cocktails by adding lemon juice. He also thought it would make a better drink if he used a special, sweeter gin, called Old Tom Gin. Old Tom Gin is hardly used anymore; drier gins have replaced it. In order to maintain the sweetness of the Collins, people started adding sugar, and now sweet and sour is predominantly used. The Tom Collins is still enjoyed by many people, and is the most requested Collins.

The Singapore Sling was introduced in the early 1900s at the Raffles Hotel in Singapore. It was one of the most popular drinks with the British civil servants who ruled the area until the mid 1940s.

Below are examples of popular stemmed and Collins glasses used for sours.

STEMMED ROCKS

WHISKEY SOUR

COUPETTE

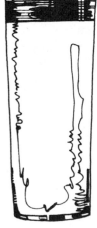

COLLINS

FROSTED COLLINS

COOLER

PREPARATIONS FOR BLENDED SOURS

1 Chill stemmed glass by filling it with ice.

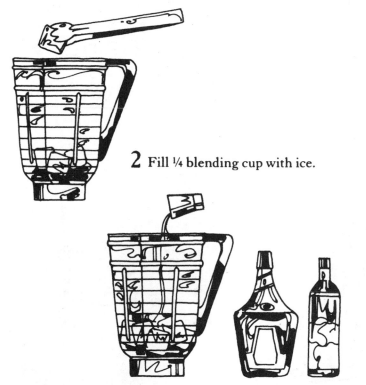

2 Fill ¼ blending cup with ice.

3 Measure liquor (liqueur) first. Add sweet and sour and any other liquid ingredients to be blended.

4 Blend

5 Remove ice from chilled glass.

6 Strain ingredients into glass.
Garnish (if any).

Bacardi Cocktail

Stemmed glass, chilled
Mixing cup, ¼ filled with ice
1 oz. Bacardi light rum
½ oz. grenadine
1½ oz. sweet and sour
Blend and strain

Between the Sheets

Stemmed glass, chilled
Mixing cup, ¼ filled with ice
½ oz. brandy
½ oz. rum
½ oz. triple sec
1½ oz. sweet and sour
Blend and strain

Daiquiri

Stemmed glass, chilled
Mixing cup, ¼ filled with ice
1 oz. light rum
2 oz. sweet and sour
Blend and strain

Daiquiri, Frozen Banana

Large stemmed glass, chilled
Mixing cup, ½ filled with
    finely crushed ice
1 oz. light rum
1½ oz. sweet and sour
½ medium ripe banana
Blend but do not strain

Daiquiri, Frozen Peach

Large stemmed glass, chilled
Mixing cup, ½ filled with
    finely crushed ice
1 oz. light rum
1½ oz. sweet and sour
¼ cup frozen or fresh peaches
Blend but do not strain

Daiquiri, Frozen Pineapple

Large stemmed glass, chilled
Mixing cup, ½ filled with
    finely crushed ice
1 oz. light rum
1½ oz. sweet and sour
4 canned pineapple rings
Blend but do not strain

Daiquiri, Frozen Strawberry

Large stemmed glass, chilled
Mixing cup, ½ filled with
    finely crushed ice
1 oz. light rum
1½ oz. sweet and sour
½ cup frozen strawberries,
    thawed
Blend but do not strain

Iguana

Stemmed glass, chilled
Mixing cup, ¼ filled with ice
½ oz. vodka
½ oz. tequila
¼ oz. coffee liqueur
1½ oz. sweet and sour
Blend and strain
Lime garnish

Jack Rose Cocktail

Stemmed glass, chilled
Mixing cup, ¼ filled with ice
1 oz. applejack
½ oz. grenadine
1½ oz. sweet and sour
Blend and strain

Malibu Wave

Stemmed glass, chilled
Mixing cup, ¼ filled with ice
1 oz. tequila
½ oz. triple sec
⅛ oz. blue curacao
1½ oz. sweet and sour
Blend and strain
Lime garnish

Margarita

Stemmed glass, with salt
   frosting on rim
(To frost with salt, moisten
   rim with lime squeeze or
   juice, and dip in dish of
   salt)
Mixing cup, ¼ filled with ice
1 oz. tequila
½ oz. triple sec
1½ oz. sweet and sour
Blend and strain

Margarita, Frozen Strawberry

Large stemmed glass, with
   either salt or sugar
   frosting, depending on
   taste (see Margarita to frost
   rim)
Mixing cup, ½ filled with
   finely crushed ice
1 oz. tequila
1½ oz. sweet and sour
½ cup frozen thawed
   strawberries
Blend but do not strain

Side Car

Stemmed glass, with sugar
   frosting on rim
(To frost with sugar, moisten
   rim with lime squeeze or
   juice, and dip in dish of
   sugar)
Mixing cup, ¼ filled with ice
1 oz. brandy
½ oz. triple sec
1½ oz. sweet and sour
Blend and strain

Stone Sour

Stemmed glass, chilled
Mixing cup, ¼ filled with ice
1 oz. apricot brandy
1 oz. orange juice
1 oz. sweet and sour
Blend and strain

Whisky Sour

Stemmed glass, chilled
Mixing cup, ¼ filled with ice
1 oz. whisky
2 oz. sweet and sour
Blend and strain
Cherry garnish

Yellow Strawberry

Stemmed glass, chilled
Mixing cup, ¼ filled with ice
1 oz. light rum
½ oz. creme de banana
4 oz. frozen thawed
   strawberries
1 oz. sweet and sour
Blend and strain
Banana slice garnish

PREPARATIONS FOR LONG SOURS

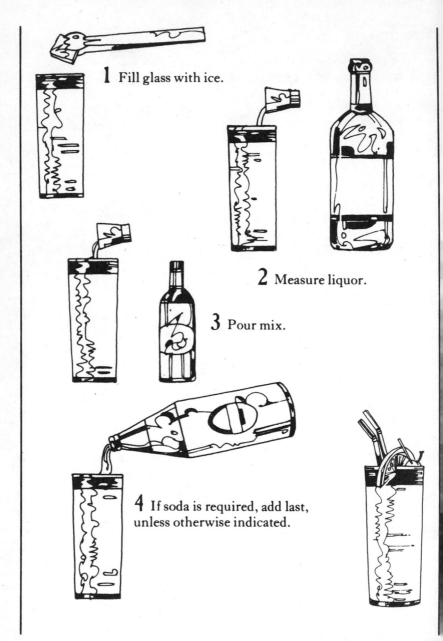

1 Fill glass with ice.

2 Measure liquor.

3 Pour mix.

4 If soda is required, add last, unless otherwise indicated.

5 Garnish (if any).

French 75

Collins glass, filled with ice
1 oz. gin
2 oz. sweet and sour
Stir well
Fill with champagne
Stir lightly

French 125

Collins glass, filled with ice
1 oz. brandy
2 oz. sweet and sour
Stir well
Fill with champagne
Stir lightly
Lemon twist garnish

Gin Fizz

Collins glass, chilled only
Mixing cup, ¼ filled with ice
1 oz. gin
2 oz. sweet and sour
Blend and strain
Fill with soda

Golden Fizz

Collins glass, chilled only
Mixing cup, ¼ filled with ice
1 oz. gin
2 oz. sweet and sour
1 egg yolk
Blend and strain
Fill with soda

Iced Tea

Collins glass, filled with ice
1 oz. vodka
1 oz. gin
½ oz. triple sec
2 oz. sweet and sour
Stir well
Splash of coke
Stir again
Lemon twist garnish

Irish Spring

Collins glass, filled with ice
1 oz. Irish whisky
½ oz. peach brandy
1 oz. orange juice
1 oz. sweet and sour
Stir well
Orange slice and cherry
　　garnishes

Joe Collins

Collins glass, filled with ice
1 oz. Scotch
2 oz. sweet and sour
Stir well
Fill with soda
Stir lightly
Cherry garnish

John Collins

Collins glass, filled with ice
1 oz. whisky
2 oz. sweet and sour
Stir well
Fill with soda
Stir lightly
Cherry garnish

Ramos Fizz

Collins glass, chilled only
Mixing cup, ¼ filled with ice
1 oz. gin
½ oz. cream
1½ oz. sweet and sour
2 dashes Orange Flower
    Water or orange juice
1 egg white
Blend and strain
Fill with soda

Royal Fizz

Collins glass, chilled only
Mixing cup, ¼ filled with ice
1 oz. gin
2 oz. sweet and sour
1 whole egg
Blend and strain
Fill with soda

Silver Fizz

Collins glass, chilled only
Mixing cup, ¼ filled with ice
1 oz. gin
2 oz. sweet and sour
1 egg white
Blend and strain
Fill with soda

Singapore Sling

Collins glass, filled with ice
½ oz. grenadine
1 oz. gin
2 oz. sweet and sour
Stir well
Fill with soda
Top with ½ oz. cherry-
    flavored brandy
Cherry garnish

Skip and Go Naked

Collins glass, filled with ice
1 oz. gin
2 oz. sweet and sour
Stir well
Fill with beer
Stir lightly

Sloe Gin Fizz

Collins glass, chilled only
Mixing cup, ¼ filled with ice
1 oz. sloe gin
2 oz. sweet and sour
Blend and strain
Fill with soda
Cherry garnish

Tom Collins

Collins glass, filled with ice
1 oz. gin
2 oz. sweet and sour
Stir well
Fill with soda
Stir lightly
Cherry garnish

Vodka Collins

Collins glass, filled with ice
1 oz. vodka
2 oz. sweet and sour
Stir well
Fill with soda
Stir lightly
Cherry garnish

TROPICAL-EXOTIC

Atlantic Breeze

Collins glass, ½ filled with ice
Mixing cup, ¼ filled with ice
1 oz. light rum
½ oz. apricot brandy
4 oz. pineapple juice
1 oz. lemon juice
Dash grenadine
Blend and strain
Top with ½ oz. Galliano
Orange slice and cherry
    garnishes

Blue Hawaii

Large stemmed glass, chilled
Mixing cup, ¼ filled with ice
½ oz. white creme de cacao
½ oz. blue curacao
1 oz. light rum
1½ oz. cream
1½ oz. pineapple juice
Blend and strain

Cherry Bomb Fireworks

Collins glass, ½ filled with ice
Mixing cup, ¼ filled with ice
½ oz. vodka
½ oz. light rum
½ oz. tequila
5 oz. Pina Colada mix, chilled
1 drop grenadine
Blend and strain
Cherry garnish

Chi Chi

Collins glass, filled with ice
Mixing cup, ¼ filled with ice
1 oz. vodka
1 oz. cream of coconut syrup
2 oz. pineapple syrup
(or, instead of syrups, 3 oz.
    Pina Colada mix)
Blend and strain
Pineapple stalk or cherry
    garnish

Fogcutter

Collins glass, filled with ice
Mixing cup, ¼ filled with ice
½ oz. brandy
½ oz. light rum
½ oz. gin
3 oz. pineapple juice
1 oz. sweet and sour
Blend and strain
Lime and lemon twist
    garnishes

Gorilla Punch

Collins glass, filled with ice
Mixing cup, ¼ filled with ice
1 oz. vodka
½ oz. blue curacao
2 oz. orange juice
2 oz. pineapple juice
Blend and strain
Cherry garnish

Ice Palace

Collins glass, filled with ice
Mixing cup, ¼ filled with ice
1 oz. light rum
½ oz. Galliano
½ oz. apricot brandy
2 oz. pineapple juice
¼ oz. lemon juice
Blend and strain
Orange section and cherry
    garnishes

Kappa Colada

Collins glass, filled with ice
Mixing cup, ¼ filled with ice
1 oz. brandy
1 oz. cream of coconut syrup
2 oz. pineapple syrup
(or, instead of syrups, 3 oz.
    Pina Colada mix)
Blend and strain
Pineapple stalk or cherry
    garnish

Mai Tai

Collins glass, filled with ice
Mixing cup, ¼ filled with ice
1 oz. light rum
½ oz. orgeat syrup
½ oz. triple sec
1½ oz. sweet and sour
Blend and strain
Cherry garnish

Navy Grog

Double rock glass, ½ filled
    with crushed ice
Mixing cup, ¼ filled with ice
½ oz. light rum
½ oz. dark rum
¼ oz. Falerum
½ oz. guava nectar
½ oz. pineapple juice
½ oz. orange juice
1 oz. sweet and sour
Blend and strain

Orange Blossom

Stemmed glass, with sugar
    frosting on rim
(To frost with sugar, moisten
    rim with lime squeeze or
    juice, and dip in dish of
    sugar)
Mixing cup, ¼ filled with ice
1 oz. gin
½ oz. simple syrup or sugar
    or, ½ oz. triple sec
1½ oz. orange juice
Blend and strain

Peach Treat

Collins glass, filled with ice
Mixing cup, ¼ filled with ice
1 oz. peach brandy
2 oz. orange juice
Blend and strain
Add 4 oz. champagne, chilled
Peach slice garnish

Pina Colada

Collins glass, filled with ice
Mixing cup, ¼ filled with ice
1 oz. light rum
1 oz. cream of coconut syrup
2 oz. pineapple syrup
(or, instead of syrups, 3 oz.
    Pina Colada mix)
Blend and strain
Pineapple stalk or cherry
    garnish

Planter's Punch

Collins glass, filled with ice
Mixing cup, ¼ filled with ice
1 oz. dark rum
½ oz. grenadine
Dash of bitters
1½ oz. sweet and sour
Blend and strain
Fill with soda
Cherry garnish

Scorpion (For 2-4 people)

Large bowl, ½ filled with ice
Mixing cup, ¼ filled with ice
1 oz. brandy
2 oz. light rum
2 oz. dark rum
2 oz. creme de almond
4 oz. sweet and sour
4 oz. pineapple juice
Blend and strain
Garnish with fruit slices

Zamboanga Hummer

Collins glass, ½ filled with ice
Mixing cup, ¼ filled with ice
½ oz. gold rum
½ oz. gin
½ oz brandy
½ oz. orange curacao
2 oz. orange juice, chilled
2 oz. pineapple juice, chilled
½ oz. lemon juice, chilled
1 tsp. brown sugar
Blend and strain

Zombie

Collins glass, filled with ice
Mixing cup, ¼ filled with ice
1 oz. light rum
½ oz. creme de almond
½ oz. triple sec
1½ oz. sweet and sour
1½ oz. orange juice
Blend and strain
Top with ½ oz. 151 proof rum
Cherry garnish

10 MARTINIS AND MANHATTANS

MARTINI HIGHLIGHTS

There are many stories about who invented the magical and mystical Martini. One source claims it was invented by a bartender in San Francisco during the California Gold Rush. A miner named Martinez had just discovered gold. To celebrate his find, he wanted a special drink other than straight whisky or beer. He asked the local bartender to make him a drink that was elegant and different in honor of his new-found wealth and status. He mentioned that the Europeans seemed to always have fancy drinks, and he felt like being fancy that day. The bartender thought for a minute and decided to mix together gin, which was very English, and vermouth, which was very French. Martinez then proceeded to go from bar to bar, buying everyone his new drink, which soon took on the name of Martini. Whether this story is true or not is a matter of speculation, but it sounds as good, if not better, than most of the ones I've heard.

The Martini definitely has its own special breed of ardent followers. Talk with several true Martini drinkers, and each will claim that they and only they really know the secret of a perfect Martini. Some claim it's the special brand of liquors they use. Others will disagree and say it's the way it's prepared that makes the difference. Still others claim it's in the secret extras they add to the recipe, such as a dash of Scotch or Spanish sherry, or a variety of other things. Whatever really makes the best Martini, it is still simply a matter of individual taste and preference.

Today's Martinis are dry vermouth and gin. However, they have gone through a drastic metamorphosis since their introduction. One of the first recorded recipes for a Martini was by Jerry Thomas, a bartender during the mid 1800s. It included 1 dash of bitters, 2 dashes of maraschino, 1 pony of Old Tom Gin, 1 wine glass of vermouth, 2 lumps of sugar, and ¼ slice of lemon. As you can see, the Martini has come a long way since Jerry was dispensing spirits.

The Martini first began to gain wide-spread popularity during the Roaring 20s. Rich socialites and businessmen thought it was their special drink, while most of the working class still enjoyed straight whiskies and beer. Recipes showed that Martinis were being made with equal portions of dry vermouth and gin. A few recipes said you could use either sweet or dry vermouth, depending on your preference. In the 1940s, the proportions began to change to two parts gin to one part dry vermouth. Sweet vermouth was out, never to be seen again in a Martini recipe. Today, popular proportions range from five parts gin to one part dry vermouth for a regular Martini, and nine to sixteen parts gin to one part dry vermouth for a dry or extra-dry Martini. Extra-dry Martinis, for all practical purposes, use one drop of dry vermouth. The term "dry," in relation to the Martini, means less vermouth.

The trend today is for Martinis to be made drier and drier. This is a shame because vermouth is an aperitif wine and has a very unique and distinct taste. As a result of there being so little vermouth in today's recipes, some Martini drinkers end up drinking practically straight gin.

I highly recommend that you not follow the masses, and, instead, experiment with different ratios of dry vermouth and gin when preparing Martinis. The perfect Martini is really a matter of personal taste.

As seen earlier, Martinis were originally made with gin. In the early 1960s, vodka was introduced, and rapidly grew in popularity. Now, almost half of the Martinis served are made with vodka instead of gin.

There are two ways to prepare a Martini—straight up, and on the rocks. Originally, almost all the Martinis were made straight up, but today, over 50 percent are made on the rocks. There are pros and cons to both methods. A straight-up Martini will have a purer taste. Since the ice is withheld during straining, the drink will stay the same strength. Conversely, a Martini on the rocks will start to get watered down as a result of the ice melting. Further, if a person wants to sip his straight-up Martini, it will eventually become warm, whereas a Martini on the rocks will stay ice cold (until all the ice melts). Again, one way is not necessarily better than the other; preparing Martinis will always be a matter of personal taste.

Classically, the Martini is served with an olive garnish. This tradition probably originated at some cocktail party, when a hungry guest took an olive hors d'oeuvre and dipped it in his drink to give the olive a little extra zest. The most popular olive used is the pimento-stuffed olive. For a change, you might want to try olives stuffed with anchovies or almonds. A lemon twist is another popular garnish for the Martini. You make a twist by totally removing the pulp of the lemon, leaving only the rind, and cutting it into approximately ¼-inch slices. To garnish the drink, hold the twist above it, with the skin side (yellow side) facing downward and the inside (white side) facing upward; twist it, and then rim the glass with the skin side. By doing this, the oils in the skin are released and allowed to spray over the drink. A lemon twist does not add to the flavor of the drink, because the oils are tasteless. However, the oils are very aromatic and add a definite aroma to the drink.

MANHATTAN HIGHLIGHTS

The Manhattan, of course, was named after Manhattan, New York. It is interesting how many drinks were originally prepared with all sorts of ingredients that are not used today. To cut the harshness of bootleg liquor, syrups and aromatic flavorings were used. A good example of this is the Manhattan. It started out having bitters, sugar, and much more vermouth in addition to the whisky (bourbon). Over the years, distilling methods have greatly improved, thus the whiskies are smoother.

The basic recipe for a Manhattan is sweet vermouth and whisky; however, there are several variations. If dry vermouth and whisky are used, it becomes a Dry Manhattan and has no sweet taste. If both dry and sweet vermouth are combined, it becomes a Perfect Manhattan and has a semisweet taste.

Some people prefer Scotch in their Manhattans instead of bourbon. This changes the name to a Scotch Manhattan, or as it is more commonly known, a Rob Roy. There was a Robin Hood-type fellow in Scotland, where Scotch is produced, whose name was Rob Roy, and so a Scotch Manhattan took on that nickname. You can make the same variations on a Rob Roy as you can on a regular Manhattan.

GLASSWARE

Below are examples of different sizes of stemmed cocktail and rock glasses that you may want to have in your home bar.

Cocktail glasses are used when making Martinis and Manhattans straight up, and, of course, rocks glasses, for when they are on the rocks.

CHAMPAGNE   COCKTAIL   COCKTAIL

STEMMED ROCKS   ROCKS

On the rocks

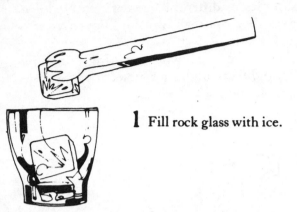

1 Fill rock glass with ice.

2 Pour vermouth first, then liquor. Garnish.

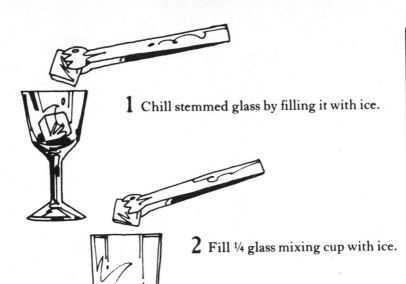

1 Chill stemmed glass by filling it with ice.

2 Fill ¼ glass mixing cup with ice.

3 Pour vermouth first, then liquor, into mixing cup with ice.

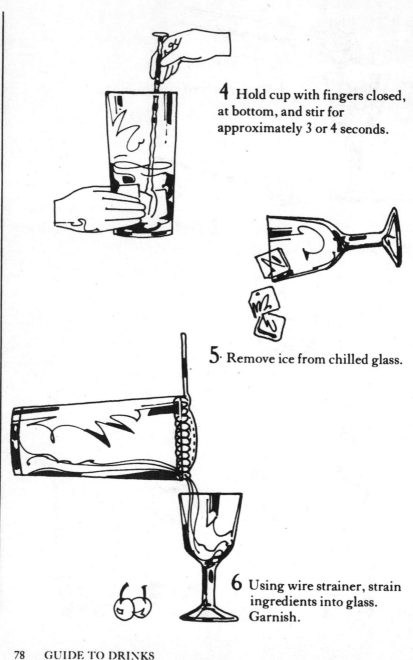

4 Hold cup with fingers closed, at bottom, and stir for approximately 3 or 4 seconds.

5. Remove ice from chilled glass.

6 Using wire strainer, strain ingredients into glass. Garnish.

Martini

Rock glass, filled with ice
Or, stemmed glass, chilled
Dash (⅛ oz.) dry vermouth
1½ oz. gin
Olive garnish

Dry to Extra Dry Martini

Rock glass, filled with ice
Or, stemmed glass, chilled
Drop (1/16 oz.) dry vermouth
1½ oz. gin
Olive garnish

Vodka Martini

Rock glass, filled with ice
Or, stemmed glass, chilled
Dash (⅛ oz.) dry vermouth
1½ oz. vodka
Olive garnish

Dry to Extra Dry Vodka Martini

Rock glass, filled with ice
Or, stemmed glass, chilled
Drop (1/16 oz.) dry vermouth
1½ oz. vodka
Olive garnish

(You may also make a Vodka Gibson. Gibson merely means that you garnish with an onion instead of an olive.)

A Different Martini:

Golden Drop Dusty; Smokey; Chicago

Preferably rock glass, filled
with ice
Can be stemmed glass, chilled
(no vermouth)
1½ oz. gin
2 drops Scotch on top, as float
Lemon twist garnish

Manhattan

Rock glass, filled with ice
Or, stemmed glass, chilled
¼ oz. sweet vermouth
1½ oz. whisky
Cherry garnish

Dry Manhattan

Rock glass, filled with ice
Or, stemmed glass, chilled
¼ oz. dry vermouth
1½ oz. whisky
Olive garnish

Perfect Manhattan

Rock glass, filled with ice
Or, stemmed glass, chilled
⅛ oz. dry vermouth
⅛ oz. sweet vermouth
1½ oz. whisky
Lemon twist garnish

Rob Roy (Scotch Manhattan)

Rock glass, filled with ice
Or, stemmed glass, chilled
¼ oz. sweet vermouth
1½ oz. Scotch
Cherry garnish

Dry Rob Roy (Dry Scotch Manhattan)

Rock glass, filled with ice
Or, stemmed glass, chilled
¼ oz. dry vermouth
1½ oz. Scotch
Olive garnish

Perfect Rob Roy (Perfect Scotch Manhattan)

Rock glass, filled with ice
Or, stemmed glass, chilled
⅛ oz. dry vermouth
⅛ oz. sweet vermouth
1½ oz. Scotch
Lemon twist garnish

Southern Comfort Manhattan

Rock glass, filled with ice
Or, stemmed glass, chilled
¼ oz. dry vermouth
1½ oz. Southern Comfort
Cherry garnish
(Dry vermouth is used to offset the sweetness of Southern Comfort)

Brandy Manhattan

Rock glass, filled with ice
Or, stemmed glass, chilled
¼ oz. sweet vermouth
1½ oz. brandy
Cherry garnish

Dry Brandy Manhattan

Rock glass, filled with ice
Or, stemmed glass, chilled
¼ oz. dry vermouth
1½ oz. brandy
Olive garnish

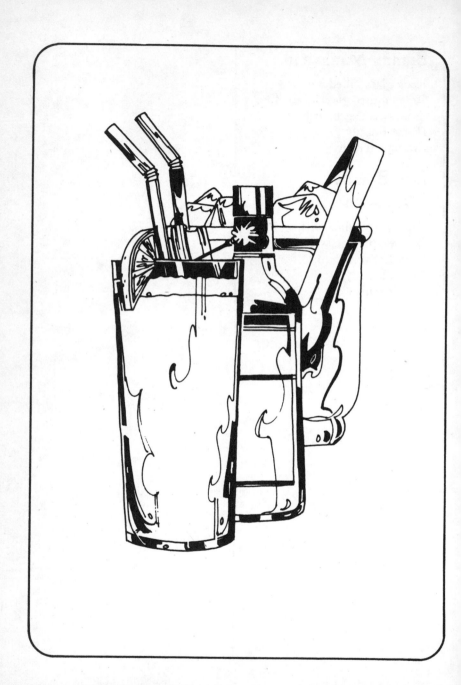

11 LIQUOR-AND-MIX DRINKS

HIGHLIGHTS

Several popular drinks containing a liquor and a non-alcoholic mix have very interesting stories behind them.

The Gin and Tonic originated in India during the late 1800s, when India was ruled by Great Britain. British troops were required to take a daily dose of a medicine called quinine to guard against the dreaded disease malaria. To offset the heavy bitterness of quinine, sugar and water were added. The mixture became known as "Indian Quinine" or "Indian Tonic Water." It wasn't too long before the innovative troops started to add their favorite liquor, gin, to the "medicine" to make it even more palatable. Today, quinine (tonic) water contains only a minute amount of quinine and has no medical value at all. The quinine is added only to give tonic water its unique bitterness. Eventually, they added the quinine and sugar to soda (carbonated water), and tonic became similar to a soft drink. Many people today drink it straight (no liquor) with a lime squeeze.

One of the first mixed drinks, the Highball, became well known in the mid 1800s. "Highball" was a railroad term. To signal fast, oncoming trains that the track was clear and there was no need to slow down, railroad men put a ball on a high pole. When the railroad men had time enough to stop for a fast drink of whisky and ginger ale (that's all they had then), they referred to it as a Highball.

Mixed drinks became especially popular during Prohibition, in the early 1920s. Bootleg liquor did not go through the extensive distillation and aging processes like that of commercial liquor. Therefore, it was of poor quality and had a harsh taste. It was usually bottled within twenty-four hours after being distilled. "Bathtub Gin," a popular expression of those times, was literally true. If you wanted a drink, you couldn't be choosy. You drank whatever your local speakeasy served and liked it, or you didn't drink at all. People quickly became experts at mixing illegal liquors with all types of mixes to improve their tastes.

In the 1940s, three drinks hit the drinking world and are still extremely popular today. The 7&7 was the brainchild of the Seagrams Distilling Company and the Seven Up Bottling Company. They ran an extensive advertising campaign giving the recipes of Seagrams Seven Crown Blended Whisky mixed with 7Up. The name 7&7 was born, and Seagrams Seven Crown Whisky became the largest selling whisky in the country for many years. The 7&7 is still one of the most widely requested mixed drinks. The Rum and Coke became a favorite drink because of a hit song by the Andrew Sisters called "Rum and Coca Cola." The Screwdriver supposedly got its name from American oil workers in Iran who were in the habit of mixing vodka with orange juice and stirring it with their screwdrivers.

The idea of using mixes with liquors has carried on through the years. Today, over half the liquor sold will be mixed with something else. To complete your home bar, you should have the following common mixes: soda water, tonic water, cola, 7Up, ginger ale, orange juice, tomato juice, grapefruit juice, and, of course, water.

Different mixes have an affinity for different liquors. Most of the dark liquors—the whiskies, such as Scotch, bourbon, and Canadian—are usually mixed with water or soda water, and occasionally ginger ale. Using water or soda water will not change the distinct flavor of the liquor. The clear liquors, such as gin, vodka, and rum are usually mixed with cola, 7Up, tonic water, or the juices. Liquor and mix companies are always coming out with new combinations. Consequently, it is becoming fashionable to mix anything with anything. As we've stated many times, drinking is very personal and depends on individual preference.

The basic concept behind adding a mix to a liquor is to cut the alcoholic bite of the drink. When heavily flavored mixes are used, such as cola and juices, the idea is to mask the liquor taste completely.

People who order their liquor and mix drinks tall, don't want to get intoxicated too quickly. They want to sit and linger over a long drink instead of having two or three short drinks in a row. They are getting more mix than liquor. Conversely, people who have doubles want, and can probably handle, more liquor and less mix. Doubles are served in a regular seven-ounce to ten-ounce highball glass, and talls in a chimney or Collins glass.

Below are examples of popular highball and Collins glasses used for liquor-and-mix drinks.

 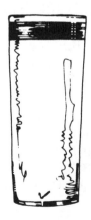 

COLLINS   FROSTED COLLINS   HIGHBALL

BLOODY MARY

The Bloody Mary is the second most requested cocktail in the nation. It's always been a favorite morning drink, especially during Sunday brunches, and many people still swear that a Bloody Mary helps relieve the pains of a hangover.

The original Bloody Mary has gone through some drastic changes since its modest beginnings in the 1940s. Gin was used instead of vodka, because vodka didn't gain full notoriety until the 1960s. Therefore, in the early 1960s, the basic recipe consisted of vodka, tomato juice, and a lime squeeze. Today, a Bloody Mary can range from having a mild tomato juice flavor (like the original), to a hot, spicy, almost burning taste (the morning eye-opener). The perfect Bloody Mary, like the perfect Martini, is a matter of individual taste and preference.

With the advent of the spicy Bloody Mary, many enterprising mix companies have developed their own versions of a Bloody Mary mix. They have added all types of herbs and spices to a tomato-juice base, so all you do is add this pre-mix to vodka and add your garnish. Each manufacturer uses different ingredients, so their tastes will vary. If you're not sure how you prefer your Bloody Mary, we suggest that you make it from scratch. This will enable you to create the perfect combination of spices that suits your taste. After you know what you like, you can then try the pre-mixes and compare. You might find that none can top what you've invented.

Below is a list of the most common ingredients used in Bloody Marys, with tomato juice as a base. After you've decided on your favorite recipe, you might want to start using different liquors, such as rum, gin, aquavit, or anything else. Several Marys made with these liquors have already acquired famous names, which you'll find in our recipe list.

Ingredients

salt
pepper
celery salt
nutmeg
worcestershire sauce
tabasco sauce (very hot)
beef bouillon
carrot juice
lemon juice
A-1 sauce
egg white

Garnishes

celery stick
carrot stick
broccoli stalk
slice of cucumber
slice of zucchini
lime squeeze
lemon squeeze

PREPARATION

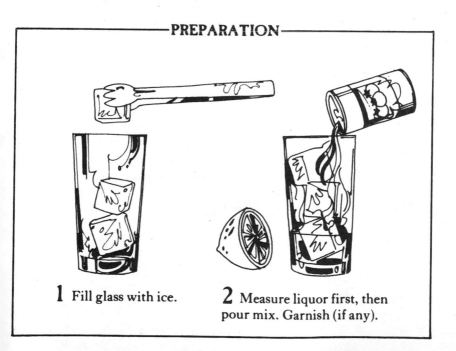

1 Fill glass with ice.

2 Measure liquor first, then pour mix. Garnish (if any).

Alabama K.O.
Alabama Slammer

Collins glass, filled with ice
½ oz. sloe gin
½ oz. creme de banana
Fill with orange juice
Stir well
Top with ½ oz. Southern
　Comfort

Bloody Bull

Highball glass, filled with ice
1 oz. vodka
½ fill with Bloody Mary mix
½ fill with beef bouillon
Stir well
Lime garnish (optional)

Bloody Maria

Highball glass, filled with ice
1 oz. tequila
Fill with Bloody Mary mix
Stir well
Celery stick or lime garnish .

Bloody Mary

Highball glass, filled with ice
1 oz. vodka
2 dashes pepper
2 dashes salt
2 dashes celery salt
4 drops worcestershire sauce
1 drop tabasco sauce
　(optional)
Fill with tomato juice
Or, fill with commercial
　Bloody Mary mix instead
　of spices and tomato juice
Stir well
Celery stick or lime garnish

Bocci Ball

Highball glass, filled with ice
1 oz. amaretto
Fill with orange juice
Stir well
Splash soda
Stir lightly

Brass Monkey

Highball glass, filled with ice
½ oz. vodka
½ oz. light rum
Fill with orange juice
Stir well

Bull Frog

Highball glass, filled with ice
1 oz. vodka
Fill with lime *Aide*
Stir well
Lime garnish

Bull Shot

Highball glass, filled with ice
1 oz. vodka
Fill with beef bouillon or,
    Bull Shot pre-mix
Stir well
Lime garnish (optional)

Candy Bar
Tootsie Roll

Highball glass, filled with ice
1 oz. Kahlua
Fill with orange juice
Stir well

Campari and Soda

Highball glass, filled with ice
1 oz. Campari
Fill with soda
Stir
Lemon twist garnish

Cuba Libra

Highball glass, filled with ice
1 oz. rum
Fill with coke
Stir
Lime garnish

Danish Mary

Highball glass, filled with ice
1 oz. akvavit (aquavit)
Fill with Bloody Mary mix
Stir well
Celery stick or lime garnish

Freddy Fudpucker
Cactus Cooler;
Cactus Banger

Collins glass, filled with ice
1 oz. tequila
Fill with orange juice
Stir well
Top with ½ oz. Galliano
Stir again, if desired

Gin Gimlet

Rock glass, filled with ice
1½ oz. gin
½ oz. Rose's lime juice
Stir well
Lime garnish

Gin and Tonic

Highball glass, filled with ice
1 oz. gin
Fill with tonic
Stir
Lime garnish

Gin Rickey

Highball glass, filled with ice
1 oz. gin
Fill with soda
Stir
Lime garnish

Greyhound

Highball glass, filled with ice
1 oz. vodka
Fill with grapefruit juice
Stir well

Harvey Wallbanger

Collins glass, filled with ice
1 oz. vodka
Fill with orange juice
Stir well
Top with ½ oz. Galliano
Stir lightly if desired

Highball

Highball glass, filled with ice
1 oz. whisky
Fill with ginger ale
Stir

Mashed Old Fashioned

In rock glass, place:
Cherry
Piece of orange
Sugar cube or 1 tsp. sugar
2 dashes bitters
Dash soda
Mash together
Fill glass with ice
Add 1 oz. bourbon
Orange slice and cherry
  garnish

Mint Julep

In collins glass, place:
6 mint leaves
½ oz. simple syrup
Mash leaves
Add 1 oz. bourbon
Fill glass with crushed ice
Add another 1 oz. bourbon
Stir well
Mint sprig garnish
(Simple syrup mix: 4 tsp.
granulated sugar and ½ oz.
water. Cook until dissolved.)

Old Fashioned

In rock glass, place:
1 sugar cube or 1 tsp. sugar
2 dashes bitters
Dash soda
Mash together
Fill glass with ice
Add 1 oz. bourbon
Cherry garnish

Panther

Rock glass, filled with ice
1½ oz. tequila
½ oz. sweet and sour
Stir well

Popsicle

Highball glass, filled with ice
1 oz. amaretto
½ fill with orange juice
½ fill with cream
Stir well

Presbyterian

Highball glass, filled with ice
1 oz. whisky
½ fill with soda
½ fill with ginger ale
Stir
Lemon twist garnish

Red Snapper

Highball glass, filled with ice
1 oz. gin
Fill with Bloody Mary mix
Stir well
Celery stick or lime garnish

Rootbeer Float

Collins glass, filled with ice
½ oz. vodka
½ oz. Galliano
½ oz. cream
Stir well
Fill with coke
Stir lightly
Top with whipped cream

Rum and Coke

Highball glass, filled with ice
1 oz. rum
Fill with coke
Stir

Salty Dog

Highball glass, with salt
   frosting on rim and filled
   with ice
(To frost with salt, moisten
   rim with lime squeeze or
   juice, and dip in dish of
   salt)
1 oz. vodka
Fill with grapefruit juice
Stir well

Scotch and Soda

Highball glass, filled with ice
1 oz. Scotch
Fill with soda
Stir
(Note: Any liquor can be
   mixed with soda)

Screwdriver

Highball glass, filled with ice
1 oz. vodka
Fill with orange juice
Stir well

Separator

Highball glass, filled with ice
1½ oz. brandy
½ oz. Kahlua
Fill with cream
Stir well

7 & 7

Highball glass, filled with ice
1 oz. Seagrams 7 Crown
   Whisky
Fill with 7Up
Stir

Slow Comfortable Screw

Collins glass, filled with ice
1 oz. sloe gin
½ oz. Southern Comfort
Fill with orange juice
Stir well

Slow Comfortable Screw Up Against the Wall

Collins glass, filled with ice
½ oz. sloe gin
½ oz. Southern Comfort
½ oz. Galliano
Fill with orange juice
Stir well

Slow Comfortable Screw Up Against the Wall, Mexican Style

Collins glass, filled with ice
½ oz. sloe gin
½ oz. Southern Comfort
½ oz. Galliano
½ oz. tequila
Fill with orange juice
Stir well

Slow Screw

Highball glass, filled with ice
1 oz. sloe gin
Fill with orange juice
Stir well

Smith and Kearns

Highball glass, filled with ice
1 oz. Kahlua
1 oz. cream
Stir well
Fill with soda
Stir lightly

Sombrero

Rock glass, filled with ice
1½ oz. Kahlua
½ oz. cream
Stir well

Tequila Sunrise

Collins glass, filled with ice
1 oz. tequila
Fill with orange juice
Stir well
Top with ½ oz. grenadine
Stir lightly if desired
Cherry garnish

Tequila Sunset

Collins glass, filled with ice
1 oz. tequila
Fill with orange juice
Stir well
Top with ½ oz. blackberry
    brandy
Stir lightly if desired
Cherry garnish

Vodka Gimlet

Rock glass, filled with ice
1½ oz. vodka
½ oz. Rose's lime juice
Stir well
Lime garnish

Whisky and Water

Highball glass, filled with ice
1 oz. whisky
Fill with water
Stir
(Note: Any liquor can be
    mixed with water)

12 TWO-LIQUOR DRINKS

HIGHLIGHTS

Two-liquor drinks have grown in popularity in the 1970s. Their overall flavor is sweet, and they were originally requested as after-dinner drinks. This has changed recently, and they are now suitable anytime.

As the name implies, two-liquor drinks follow the pattern of having a dry liquor, such as whisky, vodka, or brandy as a base, and a sweet, heavy liqueur, such as Kahlua, creme de menthe, or amaretto on top. There will always be more of the base liquor in the drink, because it only takes a small amount of the liqueur to sweeten a two-liquor drink. Too much of the liqueur will ruin the drink by making it too sweet. The combination of liquor and liqueur will usually total two ounces. The classic recipe is 1½ ounces of liquor and ½ ounce of liqueur. Consequently, these drinks are very potent, but also smooth, because of the sugar in the liqueurs.

There are over 250 different kinds of liqueurs, and distillers are constantly inventing new ones. As a result, every time a new liqueur is marketed, the companies advertise new recipes to increase sales. For example, amaretto, Kahlua, and Midori have flooded the market by promoting new drinks using their liqueur on top of something else. The liquor business is highly competitive; if their new recipes catch on, a company has it made.

With all the different liquors and liqueurs that are available, you can make an almost unlimited amount of two-liquor drinks. Don't be afraid to experiment with a liquor that you don't particularly like. Some people who don't prefer Scotch will like a Rusty Nail, which is Scotch and Drambuie. Drambuie is a Scotch-based liqueur with honey and spices. An excellent base liquor is vodka, because it doesn't have a flavor or smell. By putting a liqueur on top of vodka, you will only taste the distinct flavor of that liqueur. As you can see, there are many possible variations, so use your imagination and have fun.

Below are examples of popular rocks glasses.

ROCKS

PREPARATION

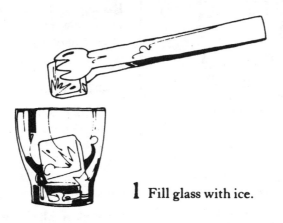

1 Fill glass with ice.

2 Measure liquor first. Top with liqueur.

Black Russian

Rock glass, filled with ice
1½ oz. vodka
½ oz. Kahlua
Stir

Brave Bull

Rock glass, filled with ice
1½ oz. tequila
½ oz. Kahlua
Stir

Dirty Mother

Rock glass, filled with ice
1½ oz. brandy
½ oz. Kahlua
Stir

Dirty White Mother

Rock glass, filled with ice
1½ oz. brandy
½ oz. Kahlua
Float cream on top
Stir

French Connection

Rock glass, filled with ice
1½ oz. brandy
½ oz. amaretto
Stir

Godfather

Rock glass, filled with ice
1½ oz. Scotch
½ oz. amaretto
Stir

Godmother

Rock glass, filled with ice
1½ oz. vodka
½ oz. amaretto
Stir

Green Dragon

Rock glass, filled with ice
1½ oz. vodka
½ oz. green creme
    de menthe
Stir

Green Hornet

Rock glass, filled with ice
1½ oz. brandy
½ oz. green creme
    de menthe
Stir

High Jamaican Wind

Rock glass, filled with ice
1½ oz. Myer's rum
½ oz. Kahlua
Float cream on top
Stir

International Stinger

Rock glass, filled with ice
1½ oz. Metaxa
½ oz. Galliano
Stir

Italian Stallion
Italian Stinger

Rock glass, filled with ice
1½ oz. brandy
½ oz. Galliano
Stir

Irish Brogue

Rock glass, filled with ice
1½ oz. Irish whisky
½ oz. Irish whisky liqueur
Stir

Jamaican Wind

Rock glass, filled with ice
1½ oz. Myer's rum
½ oz. Kahlua
Stir

Marlon Brando

Rock glass, filled with ice
1½ oz. Scotch
½ oz. amaretto
Float cream on top
Stir

Peppermint Patty

Rock glass, filled with ice
½ oz. peppermint schnapps
½ oz. brown creme de cacao
1 oz. cream
Stir

Rusty Nail

Rock glass, filled with ice
1½ oz. Scotch
½ oz. Drambuie
Stir

Scarlet O'Hara

Rock glass, filled with ice
1½ oz. Southern Comfort
½ oz. grenadine
Stir

Sicilian Kiss

Rock glass, filled with ice
1½ oz. Southern Comfort
½ oz. amaretto
Stir

Snow Shoe

Rock glass, filled with ice
1½ oz. 101 proof Wild
    Turkey Bourbon
½ oz. peppermint schnapps
Stir

Stinger

Rock glass, filled with ice
1½ oz. brandy
½ oz. white creme de menthe
Stir

Sunbeam

Rock glass, filled with ice
1½ oz. Galliano
½ oz. sweet vermouth
Stir

White Bull

Rock glass, filled with ice
1½ oz. tequila
½ oz. Kahlua
Float cream on top
Stir

White Russian

Rock glass, filled with ice
1½ oz. vodka
½ oz. Kahlua
Float cream on top
Stir

White Spider

Rock glass, filled with ice
1½ oz. vodka
½ oz. white creme de menthe
Stir

White Wing

Rock glass, filled with ice
1½ oz. gin
½ oz. white creme de menthe
Stir

13 WINE DRINKS AND PUNCHES

HIGHLIGHTS

This special group of drinks uses a wine base with mixers or a variety of ingredients. The champagne cocktail is probably the oldest, going back before Prohibition. It was a favorite of the Roaring 20s, and is still a popular brunch cocktail along with it's sister cocktail, the Mimosa.

The Negroni, Kir, and Vermouth Cassis are cocktail variations of very popular drinks in France and Italy, where most cocktails are made with a wine base rather than liquor.

The wine cooler is a drink of the 60s and 70s, in which any type of wine may be mixed with lemon/lime soft drinks.

Punches were a holiday tradition in England during the 17th century. They were also extensively popular to help celebrate weddings and other special events. What better way to entertain hundreds of people than to make up massive silver or crystal bowls filled with marinated fruits, wine, and gin, and let them brew for several days before being served.

Today, punches are a great way to serve large groups with a minimum effort and expense. A one-gallon punch bowl can serve up to ten servings and can be prepared before the guests arrive.

ROUND WINE   TALL WINE

CHAMPAGNE

Champagne Cocktail

Champagne glass, chilled
Place in glass:
1 sugar cube
1 drop bitters
Lemon twist
Fill with champagne, chilled
Variation:
1 sugar cube
2 dashes brandy
Lemon twist
Fill with champagne, chilled

Dubonnet Cocktail

Rock glass, filled with ice
Or, stemmed glass, chilled
1 oz. gin or vodka
1 oz. Dubonnet (red)
(If in stemmed glass, prepare
in glass mixing cup, stir and
strain)

Kir

Stemmed glass, with little ice
Almost fill with white wine,
   chilled
Top with ½ oz. creme
   de cassis

Mimosa

Large wine glass, chilled
½ fill with orange juice
½ fill with champagne
Stir gently

Negroni

Highball glass, filled with ice
1 oz. gin or vodka
1 oz. Campari
1 oz. sweet vermouth
Stir
Lemon twist garnish

Royal Kir

Stemmed glass, with little ice
Almost fill with champagne,
   chilled
Top with ½ oz. creme
   de cassis

Vermouth Cassis

Highball glass, filled with ice
1 oz. sweet vermouth or, 1 oz.
   dry vermouth, depending
   on taste
1 oz. creme de cassis
Fill with soda
Stir
Lemon twist garnish

White Wine Spritzer

Highball glass, ½ filled with
  ice
½ filled with white wine,
  chilled
Fill with soda
Stir gently
Lemon twist garnish

Wine Cooler

Highball glass, ½ filled with
  ice
½ filled with burgundy wine
  or, rosé wine, depending
  on taste
Fill with 7Up
Stir gently
Cherry garnish

PUNCHES

Punches are fun and are nice to have at many special
parties.

Apple Ginger Punch

18 oz. apple brandy, either
   calvados or applejack
2 oz. maraschino liqueur
2 oz. kirsch
1 quart pineapple-grapefruit
   juice
24 oz. Green-ginger Wine
1 quart plus 1 pint ginger beer
   or ginger ale
2 red apples
2 yellow apples

Chill all ingredients. Pour all
liquids except ginger beer
over large block of ice in
punch bowl. Stir well. Let
mixture ripen 1 hour in
refrigerator. Cut unpeeled
apples into wedgelike slices,
discarding core. Just before
serving, pour ginger beer into
bowl. Float apple slices on
top.

Barbados Bowl

8 medium-size ripe bananas
1 cup lime juice
1 cup sugar
12 oz. light rum
12 oz. dark rum
1 quart plus 12 oz. pineapple
   juice
12 oz. mango nectar
2 limes, sliced

Chill all ingredients except
bananas. Cut 6 bananas into

thin slices and place in
electric blender with lime
juice and sugar. Blend until
smooth. Pour over block of
ice in punch bowl. Add both
kinds of rum, pineapple juice,
and mango nectar. Stir well.
Let mixture ripen in
refrigerator 1 hour before
serving. Cut remaining 2
bananas into thin slices. Float
banana and lime slices on
punch.

Black-Cherry Rum Punch

24 oz. light rum
4 oz. 151 proof rum
4 oz. dark Jamaican rum
2 17-oz. cans pitted black
   cherries in heavy syrup
16 oz. sweet and sour
4 oz. fresh orange juice
4 oz. Peter Heering
4 oz. creme de cassis
2 limes, thinly sliced
1 quart club soda

Put all ingredients except
soda into punch bowl. Add
block of ice. Stir well.
Refrigerate 1 hour. Add soda.
Stir well.

Brandy Eggnog Bowl

12 eggs
½ cup sugar
24 oz. brandy
4 oz. dark rum
3 quarts milk
8 oz. cream
Grated nutmeg

Carefully separate egg yolks from whites. In punch bowl, combine egg yolks and sugar. Beat well with a wire whisk. Gradually add brandy, rum, milk, and cream. Beat well. Taste. Add more sugar if desired. Place the bowl in the refrigerator for at least 2 hours. Just before serving, beat egg whites in a separate bowl or in mixer, in two batches if necessary, until stiff. Fold whites into punch; that is, do not mix them with a round-the-bowl movement, but use the wire whisk in a down-over-up stroke until whites are thoroughly blended. Ladle into cups. Sprinkle with nutmeg.

Champagne Punch with Maraschino

6 oz. maraschino liqueur
6 oz. brandy
1 teaspoon orange bitters
2 oranges, thinly sliced
1 lemon, thinly sliced
4 fifths iced brut champagne

Put maraschino, brandy, orange bitters, and sliced fruit into punch bowl. Let mixture brew about 1 hour in refrigerator. Place large chunk of ice in bowl. Pour champagne over ice. Stir lightly.

Emerald Bowl

3 quarts chilled emerald
    riesling
6 oz. brandy
6 oz. apricot-flavored brandy
20 oz. chilled apple juice
16 slices cucumber peel, each
    1 inch long and ½ inch
    wide

Pour riesling, brandy, apricot brandy, and apple juice over large block of ice in punch bowl. Add cucumber peel. Stir. Refrigerate 1 hour.

Interplanetary Punch

24 oz. light rum
4 oz. dark rum
8 oz. peppermint schnapps
1 quart mango nectar
12 oz. cream
1 quart orange juice
8 large sprigs mint
1 large ripe fresh mango, if
   available
6 thin slices orange

Pre-chill all ingredients
including liquors. Place large
block of ice in punch bowl.
Add both kinds of rum,
peppermint schnapps, mango
nectar, cream, and orange
juice. Stir very well. Tear
mint leaves from stems. Peel
and cut mango into small
slices. (Canned mango may
be used in place of fresh,
however, it will not float.)
Cut orange rounds into
quarters. Float mint leaves
and fruit on punch.
Refrigerate for 1 hour.

Mountain Red Punch

3 quarts chilled California red
   wine
4 oz. amaretto
4 oz. brandy
4 oz. cherry-flavored brandy
16 oz. ginger ale
2 oz. julienne almonds,
   toasted

Pour wine, amaretto, brandy,
and cherry brandy over large
block of ice in punch bowl.
Refrigerate 1 hour. Add
ginger ale. Stir lightly. Float
almonds on top. (Note:
Almonds may be toasted by
placing in shallow pan in
moderate oven for about 10
minutes. Avoid scorching.)

Polynesian Punch Bowl

24 oz. light rum
6 oz. cream of coconut
1 quart plus 1 cup pineapple
   juice
3 cups orange juice
8 oz. sloe gin
5 oz. peppermint schnapps
1 cup lemon juice
12 thin slices very ripe fresh
   pineapple
12 thin slices orange
1 pint iced club soda

Pour rum, cream of coconut, pineapple juice, orange juice, sloe gin, peppermint schnapps, and lemon juice into punch bowl. Stir well until all ingredients, particularly cream of coconut, are well blended. Add a large block of ice and the pineapple and orange slices, and place in refrigerator for about 1 hour. Add soda, and stir lightly just before serving.

Rosé Punch

3 quarts chilled rosé wine
8 oz. cranberry liqueur
4 oz. brandy
16 thin slices pineapple
1 quart frozen thawed
   strawberries
16 oz. iced club soda

Pour wine, cranberry liqueur, and brandy over a large block of ice in a punch bowl. Add pineapple slices and strawberries. Refrigerate 1 hour. Add iced club soda. Stir lightly.

Sangria

24 oz. light dry red wine
1 whole orange
1 ripe Elberta peach, peeled
   and sliced
6 slices lemon
2 oz. brandy
1 oz. triple sec
1 oz. maraschino liqueur
1 tbsp. or more sugar to taste
10 oz. iced club soda

Cut entire peel of orange in a single strip, beginning at stem end, and continuing until spiral reaches bottom of fruit. White part should be cut along with outer peel, so that orange fruit is exposed. Leave peel attached to orange bottom, so that fruit may be suspended in pitcher. Pour wine into glass pitcher. Add peach, lemon, brandy, triple sec, maraschino liqueur, and sugar. Stir to dissolve sugar.

Carefully place orange in pitcher fastening top end of peel over rim. Let mixture marinate at room temperature at least 1 hour. Add soda and 1 tray of ice cubes to pitcher. Stir.

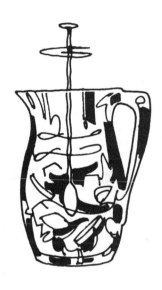

14 HOT DRINKS

HIGHLIGHTS

Hot drinks classically bring to mind cold weather, ski resorts, fireplaces, and illness remedies. These ideas are not true anymore. Now, hot drinks are enjoyed any time of the day, month, and year. Many people have coffee drinks on a lazy weekend, during the late morning, or settle down with a good book and a hot toddy before retiring at night. Hot drinks are smooth and comforting, but be aware that when alcohol is mixed with a hot liquid, it goes through the blood stream faster. Coffee will not offset the effect of alcohol. In fact, if you drink coffee thinking it will help you get sober, it won't; you'll just be wide awake. The only thing that aids in the sobering process is time. It takes an hour for every ounce of alcohol to pass entirely through the body. Enjoy hot drinks, but keep in mind that they are just as powerful as any other cocktail, if not more.

When liquor is added to a hot liquid, the alcohol will quickly cool the hot coffee or water. Ideally, the drink should be served hot, but not scalding. The best way to achieve this is to heat it in a saucepan or chafing dish. Do not boil, or the alcohol will evaporate. Let cool for a minute before serving.

PREPARATIONS FOR HOT DRINKS

If using a glass for hot drinks, be sure to place a metal spoon in the glass before pouring hot liquid. The spoon absorbs the heat and prevents the glass from breaking.

In coffee drinks, sugar is called for in some, but not all, of the recipes. Sugar is not needed when using a liqueur, as the liqueur already contains a sufficient amount of sugar. Liquor and coffee, however, is a somewhat harsh combination. Adding sugar to these drinks cuts the alcoholic bite, thereby making the drinks smoother.

PREPARATIONS FOR IRISH COFFEE

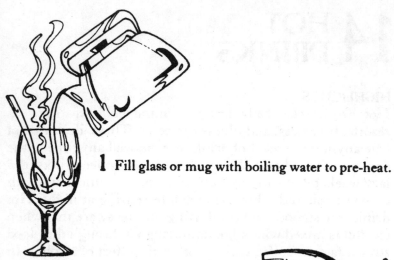

1 Fill glass or mug with boiling water to pre-heat.

2 Leave water in glass for approximately 30 seconds and remove.

3 Put sugar in glass or mug.

4 Measure liquor into glass or mug.

5 Fill with hot coffee.

6 Top with whipped cream.

HANDLED MUG

GOBLET

MICHELOB TANKARD

TANKARD

Apple Grog

1½ oz. apple jack
½ oz. 151-proof rum
1 tbsp. brown sugar
4 oz. water
2 whole allspice
1 piece stick cinnamon
2-inch strip lemon peel

Pour applejack, sugar, and water into saucepan. Add allspice and cinnamon. Bring to boiling point, but do not boil. Pour into preheated mug. Twist lemon peel above mug and drop into drink. Float rum on top.

Blackberry Demitasse

1 oz. blackberry liqueur or
    blackberry brandy
½ oz. brandy
1 tbsp. blackberry jelly
½ oz. water
½ tsp. lemon juice
¼ thin slice lemon

Heat blackberry liqueur, jelly, brandy, water, and lemon juice without boiling. Stir well until jelly is completely dissolved. Pour into demitasse cup. Add lemon slice.

Calypso Coffee

Coffee mug
½ oz. light rum
½ oz. coffee liqueur
Fill with hot coffee
Top with whipped cream

Cappuccino Vivace

¼ oz. brandy
¼ oz. light rum
¼ oz. gin
¼ oz. white creme de cacao
¼ oz. Galliano
4 oz. hot coffee
4 oz. cream
1½ tsp. instant hot chocolate
    mix

In a saucepan, mix hot coffee, cream, and hot chocolate mix. Heat but do not boil. In a separate container, mix brandy, rum, gin, creme de cacao, and galliano. Pour liquor mixture into 10-oz. stemmed glass or large mug. Add heated coffee mixture. Top with whipped cream. Note: If using stemmed glass, avoid breakage by placing a metal spoon in glass before pouring coffee mixture. The spoon absorbs the heat.

Dutch Coffee

Coffee mug
1 oz. Vandermint
Fill with hot coffee
Top with whipped cream

Hot Buttered Rum

1 oz. light rum
½ oz. dark Jamaican rum
2 whole cloves
2 whole allspice
1 inch stick cinnamon
1 tsp. sugar
1 tsp. sweet butter
Boiling water

Put the cloves, allspice, stick
cinnamon, and sugar into a
mug with a tbsp. or two of
boiling water. Let the
mixture stand 5 minutes. Add
both kinds of rum, 2 oz.
boiling water, and butter. Stir
until butter dissolves. Add
more sugar if desired.

Hot Coconut Coffee

Coffee mug
1 oz. CocoRibe
Fill with hot coffee
Top with whipped cream

Hot Peppermint Patty

1 oz. peppermint schnapps
½ oz. dark creme de cacao
1 tsp. green creme de menthe
1 packet instant hot chocolate
    mix
Whipped cream

Into coffee mug, pour
schnapps and creme de cacao.
Stir until mixed. Add packet
of hot chocolate mix. Stir
until dissolved. Almost fill
with boiling water. Stir well.
Top with whipped cream and
drizzle creme de menthe over
it.

Hot Toddy

1 oz. bourbon
4 oz. boiling water
1 tsp. sugar
3 whole cloves
1 inch stick cinnamon
1 thin slice lemon
Ground nutmeg

Into a heavy mug, put the sugar, cloves, stick cinnamon, and slice of lemon. Add 1 oz. of the boiling water. Stir well. Let the mixture stand about 5 minutes. Add the bourbon and the remaining 2 oz. boiling water. Stir. Sprinkle lightly with nutmeg.

Irish Coffee

Coffee mug
1 sugar cube
1 oz. Irish whisky
Fill with hot coffee
Top with whipped cream

Italian Coffee

Coffee mug
1 oz. anisette
Fill with hot coffee
Top with whipped cream

Jamaican Coffee

Coffee mug
1 oz. Tia Maria
Fill with hot coffee
Top with whipped cream

Kioki Coffee

Coffee mug
½ oz. brandy
½ oz. Kahlua
Fill with hot coffee
Top with whipped cream

Mexican Coffee

Coffee mug
½ oz. tequila
½ oz. Galliano
Fill with hot coffee
Top with whipped cream

Scotch Coffee

Coffee mug
1 oz. Drambuie
Fill with hot coffee
Top with whipped cream

Simmering Plum

1 oz. plum brandy (Slivovitz,
    Quetsch, or Mirabelle)
1 oz. white creme de menthe
5 oz. hot black tea
1 tsp. sugar (or more to taste)
½ oz. heavy cream
1 piece stick cinnamon
Ground coriander

In saucepan, stir tea, plum
brandy, creme de menthe,
sugar, and cream. Heat to
boiling point, but do not boil.
Pour into warm 10-oz. mug
with stick cinnamon. Stir.
Sprinkle coriander on top.

Snowberry

1 oz. strawberry liqueur
1 oz. vodka
½ oz. kirschwasser
½ oz. rock-candy syrup, or
    simple syrup
1 oz. lemon juice
5 oz. water
½ large strawberry, cut in half
    lengthwise
1 thin slice lemon

In saucepan, heat strawberry
liqueur, vodka, rock-candy
syrup, lemon juice, and water
to boiling point, but do not
boil. Pour into warm 10-oz.
mug. Dip strawberry into
rock-candy syrup. Float
lemon slice, strawberry half,
and kirschwasser on drink.

Spanish Coffee

Coffee mug
½ oz. brandy
½ oz. coffee liqueur
Fill with hot coffee
Top with whipped cream

Venetian Coffee

Coffee mug
1 sugar cube
1 oz. brandy
Fill with hot coffee
Top with whipped cream

15 LIQUEUR DRINKS

HIGHLIGHTS

Liqueur drinks have always been served after dinner. However, more and more people are requesting them anytime, and on the rocks, which makes liqueurs before lunch or dinner drinks. The days of social drinking mores are over. Now it is acceptable to have what you want, when you want it. However, liqueur drinks do seem to be the perfect highlight of a fine dinner. Many people order a mixed liqueur drink, such as a Jellybean, or just a straight liqueur, and a cup of coffee. Coffee makes an excellent chaser for liqueurs; the flavors complement each other nicely. Some people just pour the liqueur into the coffee.

Because there are so many liqueurs on the market, you can make many variations of these drinks. Liqueurs differ in weight and can therefore be floated on top of each other. Keeping this in mind, you can experiment and create your own version of the Traffic Light or a Pousse Cafe.

To float a liqueur, hold a bar spoon upside down, above the glass, and pour the liqueur over the back part of the spoon. Do this slowly so the spoon breaks the fall of the fluid, and will allow it to gently settle on top of the other liqueur.

Below are examples of liqueur glasses and a brandy snifter.

LIQUEUR

BRANDY SNIFTER

PREPARATIONS FOR LIQUEUR DRINKS

Floating Liqueurs

1 Pour heaviest liqueur into glass first.

2 Float next heaviest liqueur on top of first, with bar spoon.

Continue floating in this manner until desired look is accomplished.

Angel Tip

Liqueur glass or brandy
   snifter
¾ oz. brown creme de cacao
Float ¼ oz. cream on top
Cherry garnish

B & B

Liqueur glass or brandy
   snifter
½ oz. brandy
½ oz. Benedictine

Good and Plenty

Liqueur glass or brandy
   snifter
½ oz. ouzo
½ oz. anisette

Green Lizard

Liqueur glass or brandy
   snifter
½ oz. Bacardi 151 Proof Rum
½ oz. Green Chartreuse

Harbor Light

Liqueur glass or brandy
   snifter
½ oz. Metaxa
½ oz. Galliano

Jellybean

Liqueur glass or brandy
   snifter
½ oz. anisette
½ oz. blackberry brandy

Kamakazi

Shot or liqueur glass, chilled
Glass mixing cup, ¼ filled
   with ice
¾ oz. vodka
¼ oz. lime juice
Stir and strain
Variation:
½ oz. vodka
¼ oz. triple sec
¼ oz. lime juice

King Alphonse

Liqueur glass or brandy
 snifter
¾ oz. brown creme de cacao
Float ¼ oz. cream on top

Lion Tamer

Shot or liqueur glass, chilled
Glass mixing cup, ¼ filled
 with ice
¾ oz. Southern Comfort
¼ oz. lime juice
Stir and strain

Pousse Cafe

Liqueur glass
½ oz. green creme de menthe
Float ⅓ oz. Galliano
Float ⅓ oz. blackberry
 liqueur

Variation:
⅓ oz. banana liqueur
Float ⅓ oz. Peter Heering or
 Cherry Karise
Float ⅓ oz. cognac

Variation:
¼ oz. grenadine
Float ¼ oz. brown creme
 de cacao
Float ¼ oz. Drambuie
Float ¼ oz. sweet cream,
 flavored with creme de
 menthe

Variation:
⅓ oz. grenadine
Float ⅓ oz. brown creme
 de cacao
Float ⅓ oz. triple sec

Red Tiger

Liqueur glass or brandy
 snifter
¼ oz. sloe gin
¼ oz. tequila
¼ oz. Green Chartreuse
Top with Bacardi 151
 Proof Rum

Traffic Light

Liqueur glass or brandy
 snifter
⅓ oz. green creme de menthe
Float ⅓ oz. creme de banana
Float ⅓ oz. sloe gin

Turkey Shooter

Liqueur glass or brandy
 snifter
¾ oz. 101 Proof Wild Turkey
 Bourbon
¼ oz. white creme de menthe

16 KNOWING LIQUORS

WHISKY

Whisky is a spirit, aged in wood, obtained from the distillation of a fermented mash of grain. Whisky is produced in four countries: the United States, Canada, Scotland, and Ireland. In the last ten years, the Japanese have produced whisky for exportation, but to date it has not become a major product in the international market. The whiskies produced in Canada, Ireland, and Scotland take on the name of their countries. Whiskies produced in other countries, even though they may taste similar, cannot legally be called Canadian, Irish, or Scotch.

Whiskies vary in alcoholic strength, from 110 proof American bottled in bond whisky, to 70 proof Canadian whiskies, sold only in Canada. Most whiskies sold in the United States are either 86 or 80 proof, depending on the distiller and brand. Prior to the 1960s, most whiskies were bottled at a higher proof. Today, modern drinkers prefer lighter-tasting whiskies. Federal law requires that the label on each bottle be plainly marked with the proof of the liquor. Proof indicates the amount of alcohol in any distillate, and represents 50 percent alcohol by volume. The term "proof" came out of the pioneering era of distillation. In the beginning, to determine the strength of liquors, distillers would mix equal quantities of the spirit and gunpowder and then apply a flame to the mixture. If the gunpowder failed to burn, the spirit was too weak; if it burned too brightly, it was too strong. However, if it burned evenly, with a blue flame, it was said to have been proved. Hence the word proof. Pure alcohol, like the kind used in laboratories, is 200 proof, being 100 percent alcohol. A combination of half alcohol and half water is scored as

100 proof or 50 percent alcohol. Keep in mind that proof is a measure of alcoholic strength, not necessarily of quality.

Four steps are necessary in the production of whisky: mashing, fermenting, distilling, and aging.

Whisky is made from any type of grain, but corn, rye, wheat, and barley are the grains most commonly used. After the grain is cleaned, it is ground into meal. The meal is then cooked with water to release the starch. Then dried barley malt is added. The enzymes in the malt convert the grain starch to maltose or grain sugar. This whole process is called mashing.

The next step is fermentation. The mash is put into a large tank called a fermenter. Yeast is added, which consumes the sugar and produces alcohol. This takes from two to four days. The fermented mixture is called "beer" or "distiller's beer."

Just as you learned in science class how distilled water is made, the same method is employed in the production of whisky. The fermented mixture, "beer," is heated to boil the alcohol, but not the water. The steam from the boiled alcohol rises and is trapped. The vapors condense and become whisky. By U.S. law, whisky must be distilled at less than 190 proof or about 95 percent alcohol. It cannot be distilled at a higher proof because it would lose all the characteristics of the grain used and become a tasteless neutral spirit. Most whisky is distilled from 140 to 160 proof and some as low as 125 proof. Some of the impurities, but not all, are removed through distillation; therefore, the colorless whisky is still very harsh. Occasionally, distillers will perform the old practice of leaching—passing the whisky through charcoal.

After distillation, the whisky is diluted with deionized (demineralized) water and then aged. Aging takes place in charred oak barrels. It is said that aging is the most important step in making fine whisky, because there is no substitution for time. As the years pass, the oak gives whisky its color, the char absorbs impurities, and time alone mellows the harshness. The finished product is smooth and has a rich bouquet. The character of whisky depends on the length of time it is aged. Heavy-bodied whiskies are aged for a long time, eight years or more, whereas light-bodied whiskies are aged for four years. Aging does not make a poor whisky good, and if aged too long, it can absorb undesirable wood flavors. Whisky can only be aged in a barrel; once bottled, it stays the same forever until opened.

AMERICAN WHISKY

American whiskies are rigidly defined by law, and governed accordingly. They include bourbon, corn, sour mash, Tennessee, blended, straight, bottled in bond, and rye.

The history of American whisky and America parallel each other. Whisky was an integral part of everyday life in the Colonial days. It helped comfort the settlers during hard times and was enjoyed at the end of a rough day. It was also used to cure snakebites, ward off disease, and ease pain both superficially and internally.

The first settlers did not drink whisky. The pilgrims leaned more toward wine and beer and, later, rum. The production and consumption of whisky did not become prevalent until the Scottish and Irish immigrants settled in Pennsylvania. They fancied the taste of whisky and brought to their new country their knowledge of distillation, which was handed down from generation to generation for hundreds of years. Whisky became popular because it was easily produced; almost every farmer grew grain crops. If farmers had problems shipping their grain to market and therefore couldn't sell it, they couldn't survive. This happened often, due to lack of roads and bad weather. They quickly learned how to distill portions of their crops. Whisky sold well and was less bulky to ship than grain.

Bourbon The type of whisky, what it is called, and its flavor, depend on which grain is used. In order to be called bourbon, it must contain 51 percent corn; it must be distilled at a proof not exceeding 160; and it must be aged in new charred, white oak barrels for at least two years. Bourbon is produced only in the United States under U.S. Federal Law. Although bourbon was originally made in Bourbon County, Kentucky, it is now manufactured throughout the United States.

Corn Although corn whisky is made from corn, as is bourbon, the two differ. Corn whisky must be made from 80 percent corn mash and may be aged in used uncharred barrels.

Sour mash The difference between sour mash and other whiskies is in the fermenting process. The yeast mash is soured with a lactic culture (like sourdough bread), for a minimum of six hours. The fermented mash must contain at least 25 percent of the screened residue from the whisky still, and the fermenting time must be at least 72 hours.

Tennessee Tennessee whisky is not bourbon, although the two are very similar. Their difference lies in the extra steps taken after distillation. The whisky is seeped very slowly through vats packed with charcoal. The charcoal comes from the Tennessee highlands hard maple tree. Following the leaching process, the whisky is placed into charred, white oak barrels to be aged in the Tennessee hills.

Blended Blended whiskies are balanced and light-bodied. A variety of straight whiskies and grain neutral spirits which complement each other are blended together to develop a composite flavor characteristic that will always be uniform. U.S. Government regulations specify that blends must contain at least 20 percent straight whisky on a proof gallon basis and be bottled at not less than 80 proof. As many as 75 different straight whiskies and grain neutral spirits go into premium blends. Great care is taken in choosing special whiskies for blends. The whiskies are not just mixed, but rather allowed to sit and thoroughly blend together for a length of time known as the "marrying period."

Straight Straight whisky is distilled at no more than 160 proof and aged at least two years in new charred oak barrels. It can be produced from corn, rye, barley, or wheat grains.

Bottled in bond Bottled in bond whisky is a straight whisky, usually bourbon or rye, and is produced under U.S. Government supervision. The words "bottled in bond" do not necessarily guarantee superior whiskies, but they are normally very good. The government requires that the whisky be at least four years old, bottled at 100 proof, produced in one distillery (by the same distiller), and stored and bottled in a bonded warehouse under government supervision.

Rye For whisky to be called rye whisky, it must contain 51 percent rye grain. It must be distilled at no higher proof than 160 and aged in new charred oak barrels.

Canadian whisky Canadian whisky is a distinctive product of Canada made under government supervision in accordance with the regulations governing the manufacture of whisky in Canada. Canadian whiskies are whisky blends. The most distinguishing characteristic of Canadian whisky is its light body.

Many think that Canadian whisky is made from rye grain. Actually, it contains mostly Canadian corn with a lesser amount of rye, wheat, and barley malt. These grains are developed to withstand the rigorous Canadian climate and are slightly different from American grains. This probably contributes to the special flavor of Canadian whiskies. The proportions of the grains used in the formulas are trade secrets and vary with each distiller. It is said that Canadian whisky is unique because of these secret formulas, the production methods, and Canadian water.

Canadian blends are not made of straight whiskies and neutral spirits as are those made in the United States. Their lightest spirits, distilled at 185 proof, would be legally defined as whisky, rather than as neutral spirits, in the United States.

Canadian whisky for consumption in Canada is bottled at 70 proof. When it is bottled for export to the United States, it is bottled at 86.6 and 80 proof. It is usually six years old when bottled; if it is less than four years old, its age must be marked on the label.

The Canadian distiller is subject to more government supervision and control than any other manufacturer or privately owned enterprise in the nation. Government officers are stationed in Canadian distilleries and their control extends from the receipt of grain at the distillery, through the production process, bottling and shipping, and terminates with the payment of excise duty. There is no government interference however, with the distilling techniques employed by individual distillers. Each one has complete control over the quality and character of his products.

Irish whisky Irish whisky is a distinctive product of Ireland that is manufactured in compliance with strict laws and contains no distilled spirits less than three years old.

Some sources maintain that the making of whisky in Ireland goes back at least one thousand years. Irish whisky is blended, deriving its individual personality from the native barley grain. It is made in traditional pot stills and blended with pure, soft Irish water that has a very low mineral content. It is the only whisky in the world that is distilled three times. Only the choice center part of the distillate is retained each time, yielding spirits with a smooth, clean flavor. Irish whisky is heavier and more full bodied than Scotch and is usually 86 proof.

Scotch whisky Scotch whisky is a distinctive product of Scotland, made in compliance with the laws of Great Britain. Almost all Scotch whiskies sold in the United States are blends of malt and grain whiskies; as many as thirty different kinds are used to produce some of the better-known brands. Unblended Scotch is made, has a heavier taste, and usually remains in Scotland.

The production of Scotch malt whisky begins with careful selection of the barley. After being cleaned, it is soaked in warm water for approximately sixty hours and then allowed to dry for ten days or so, until it begins to sprout. The sprouted barley is then spread out on huge screens over peat-moss fires (similar to cooking steaks on a charcoal grill). The aroma of the smoke permeates the barley, which gives Scotch its unique smoky flavor. After being dried for several weeks, the malt is cleaned and ground into meal. The meal is mashed, and yeast is added. Then fermentation takes place, and the resulting liquid is called "wash" beer.

The Scots use a different distilling process than the Americans. An old-fashioned pot still is used instead of a continuous still. A pot still is a huge copper pot with a closed top, shaped like an inverted funnel. Its spout is bent into a right angle and tapers off in a cooling coil.

Scotch produced in separate parts of Scotland will vary due to local weather conditions, different water and peat, and traditional distilling practices of individual distilleries.

BRANDY
Brandy is a potable spirit, distilled from a fermented mash of grapes or other fruit. Most brandy is distilled from wine.

White wine, made from white grapes, is used most often. Wine that has recently finished its fermentation process makes the best brandy. An aged wine, even if it is of superior quality, won't make a good brandy.

A Dutch sea captain had a lot of wine to ship from France to Holland and not enough cargo space on his ship. He thought he could save space if he distilled the wine and just added the evaporated water back to the distilled wine when he reached Holland. Before he got a chance to add the water, his friends tried the distilled wine and liked it better that way. They called it *Brandewijn*, which means "burnt wine."

Brandies are produced wherever grapes are grown. Cognac comes from France, and Metaxa is from Greece. Brandies produced in California must be made from California grapes, and they have to meet rigid standards set by the distillers. California brandies account for over 75 percent of the brandy sales in the United States.

In many parts of Europe, brandy is made from fruit. Kirsch, from Germany, is cherry flavored, and Mirabelle, from France, has a plum flavor. To the brandy base, which contains the alcohol, they add an extract or concentrate of the fruit and sweetening syrups. The labels on fruit brandies must indicate the kind of fruit used, such as apricot brandy, cherry brandy, peach brandy, or blackberry brandy, etc. Almost all brandies are aged in oak barrels from three to eight years.

Cognac should be mentioned more specifically because it is the most famous of all the brandies. It is produced in the Cognac region of France, which is an area north of Bordeaux, bordering the Atlantic Ocean, with the city of Cognac near its center. The region is divided into seven districts, ranking in order of the quality of the cognac made in each district. In order, they are: Grande Champagne, Petite Champagne, Borderies, Fins, Bois, Bons Bois, Bois Ordinaires, and Bois a Terrior.

It is important to understand that all cognac is brandy, but not all brandy is cognac. A brandy may only be called cognac if it is distilled from wine made of the grapes that grow within the legal limits of Charente and Charente Inferieure Departments of France. Brandies distilled from wines other than these are not legally entitled to the name cognac, even though they may be shipped from the city of Cognac.

GIN

Gin is distilled from grain and receives its unique flavor and aroma from juniper berries and other botanicals. Every gin producer has his own special recipe which is under strict quality control. The flavor of gin will vary with the distiller.

Gin was first produced in Holland by Dr. Sylvius, a Dutch physician, during the 17th century. He named it Genievre, the French word for the juniper berry. It was the English who shortened the name to gin. Brought from Holland into England by English soldiers, who called it "Dutch Courage", gin soon became the national drink of England and has so remained.

Gin can be made two ways, by either being distilled or compounded. All leading popular brands sold in the United States are distilled. Compounded simply means a mixture of neutral spirits with juniper berries. Distilled gin is distilled completely.

Virtually all gins in the United States use the word "dry." You will see it on brand labels that may read, "Dry Gin," "Extra Dry Gin," "London Dry Gin," or "English Dry Gin," but they all mean the same thing—lacking in sweetness. Originally, "London Dry" meant gin produced in London, but the name "London" is considered to be generic, and therefore it is often used to describe gins produced in the United States.

There are two factors that differentiate English and American gins. First, English gin is distilled at a lower proof than American. This leaves the English gin with more of the character of the grains used. Although English gin is distilled at a lower proof, it is generally bottled at a higher proof than American gin. The other factor is the water, which influences the character of the fermented mash and the spirits distilled from that mash. Gin produced in England is usually slightly heavier in body because of these factors.

On occasion, you may see Holland or Geneva gin sold in liquor stores. These are imported from Holland and they are highly flavored and rich in aromatic oils. They have a heavy taste and do not mix well with other ingredients.

RUM

Rum is produced wherever sugar cane grows. Many countries, such as the United States, South Africa, and even Russia, produce rum, but it is only the Caribbean Islands that produce rum in quantities sufficient for worldwide export.

The islands in the Caribbean each produce a distinctive type of rum, the result of the base material used, the method of distillation, and the length of maturation. Generally, the islands where the Spanish language is spoken, such as Puerto Rico, produce light, dry-tasting rums. The English-speaking Caribbean islands produce dark, heavy-tasting rums.

By definition, rum is any alcoholic distillate made from the fermented juice of sugar cane, sugar cane syrup, sugar cane molasses, or other sugar cane by-products, distilled at less than 190 proof, that also possesses the taste, aroma, and characteristics generally attributed to rum.

Sugar cane was brought to the Caribbean by Christopher Columbus on his journey from the Azores Islands. The climate was perfect for growing sugar cane, and soon it was being grown on every Caribbean island. The Spanish colonists who followed Columbus brought with them the art of distilling and began distilling the juice of the sugar cane into an alcoholic beverage, which became known as rum. Most authors believe the word "rum" is derived from the old words rumbullion (rumpus) or rumbustion (uproar), certainly appropriate words when referring to the first rum drinkers.

Rums can be broken down into various classifications. The light-bodied ones are dry and have only a very light molasses taste. They are available in two varieties: white, which is by far the most popular, and gold, which is a mixture of light and dark. The gold is sweeter and has a more pronounced molasses taste. The two favorite light rums come from Puerto Rico and the Virgin Islands. Another classification is heavy-bodied rums that are much darker and sweeter. They have a pungent bouquet and a heavy molasses taste. The dark rums differ because of slower fermentation and special maturation processes. Well-known dark rums come from Jamaica, Demerara, Martinique, Trinidad, and New England.

TEQUILA

Tequila, the primary spirit of Mexico, has its own special flavor that is almost tart and leaves the tongue clean and tingling. In the 1970s, tequila became the fastest growing spirit in sales, as vodka did in the 1960s.

Tequila is obtained from the distillation of the fermented juice (sap) of the mescal plant, called pulque. The only source for Tequila is the mescal plant, which is a species of the agave plant. It is a cactus that takes between twelve and thirteen years to mature. Its long leaves, or spikes, are cut off at harvest time, leaving only the bulbous central core, called the pina, meaning pineapple. The pinas, which weigh from 80 pounds to 175 pounds each, are taken to the distillery where they are cooked in pressure cookers for several hours. They are then cooled and shredded, and the juice is pressed out. This liquid, along with some of the fibrous pulp, is mixed with sugar, and the mash is fermented for about four days. After fermentation, the pulque is distilled in pot stills to give low-grade alcohol which will be sold as mescal. In order to make tequila, the spirit must be redistilled to obtain the pure colorless liquor. The tequila is than aged in oak barrels for approximately 35 to 56 days. Gold tequila is left for nine months or more in fifty-gallon oak barrels that give it its color. Premium tequila is aged for over three years.

The ancient Aztecs fermented the sap of the mescal long before the arrival of the Spanish, and used the drink for ceremonial purposes. When the Spanish conquistadors arrived in Mexico, they brought with them the art of distilling. Not having grapes or grain to use, they turned to the native pulque. In crude stills they produced a rough spirit, now called mescal or mezcal. As time passed, more sophisticated techniques were introduced by a group around the small Mexican town of Tequila.

All tequila sold in the United States is produced in the area around the city of Tequila, in the state of Jalsco, Mexico. If it is produced elsewhere, the drink is called mezcal. Tequila is shipped to the United States in bulk.

VODKA

Today, vodka is the largest-selling spirit in the United States. In 1951, vodka was almost an unknown liquor in that country; only 57,000 gallons were produced. In 1979, over 21 million gallons were produced in the United States that accounted for 24 percent of the total amount of spirits sold.

Vodka mixes well with anything and everything, and because of this, became increasingly popular. It owes much of its success to what it doesn't taste like rather than what it does taste like. Vodka has virtually no taste or aroma. If mixed with orange juice, the drink will taste like orange juice. If mixed with tomato juice, the tomato juice flavor will predominate. Its neutrality does not let it interfere with the flavor of the main ingredient.

Like whisky, vodka is distilled from a fermented mash of grain, but they differ in the methods of distillation. Whisky is distilled at a low proof to retain flavor. Vodka, however, is distilled at a high proof, 190 or above, and then processed even further to remove all flavor. Most American distillers filter their vodkas through activated charcoal. Also, whisky is aged, and vodka is not.

Many people mistakenly believe that vodka is made from potatoes. It definitely is not. To reiterate, vodka is made from grain, the most common being corn, rye, and wheat.

There are many countries that claim they invented vodka, among them Poland and Russia. Some historians claim the Poles were producing it as early as the 8th century A.D., for use as medicine. It wasn't until the 15th century A.D., that both the Poles and the Russians were drinking it every day.

17 KNOWING LIQUEURS

Liqueurs are made by mixing or redistilling neutral spirits with fruits, flowers, herbs, seeds, roots, plants, or juices to which sweetening has been added.

The words liqueur and cordial are synonymous, according to the U.S. Federal Code. Originally, cordials were made in Italy and liqueurs were made in France, but this is not true today. No matter what term you prefer, U.S. Law requires that they contain a minimum of 2½ percent sugar or dextrose, or a combination, by weight. Although 2½ percent is the minimum, many liqueurs will have considerably more sugar or dextrose added. In fact, liqueurs of the same type, but made by different distillers, will vary in their degrees of sweetness.

The history of liqueurs is a varied and interesting one. The process of distilling water and aromatic liquids was known by the ancient Greeks long before the birth of Christ. The Arabs are credited with discovering the techniques of modern distilling in about A.D. 900. Spirits were gradually modified by the addition of sweet syrups and various herbs and flowers to enhance the flavor. In the Middle Ages, religious orders constantly experimented with liqueurs, adding every conceivable ingredient possible hoping to find the elixir of life. The modern inventor of liqueurs as we know them today, was Arnau de Vilanova, a physician and chemist born in 1240. He was the first to record recipes of alcohol and publicize those recipes for the healing liqueurs. He began with a sweetened spirit and started adding lemon, rose, orange flower, and gold. Gold at that time was considered the panacea for every affliction. When the Black Death came to Europe and killed over half of the population, liqueurs mixed with vegetable balms, tonics, and gold were highly treasured medicines, available only to religious orders and very wealthy nobility. Today, many modern miracle drugs contain properties of early liqueurs. Creme de menthe is often ordered after a heavy meal to freshen the palate and aid in digestion.

Liqueurs are produced wherever distilled spirits are made. Every country has its own special liqueur; Mexico has Kahlua, Scotland has Drambuie, Italy has Galliano, Ireland has Irish Mist, Jamaica has Tia Maria, France has Benedictine, to name a few.

There are three basic methods in the production of liqueurs: percolation, maceration, and distillation.

Percolation uses the same principle that is involved in preparing your morning coffee. When producing liqueurs, a large tank is used. The spirits are placed at the bottom, and the fruit, in a basketlike container, is placed at the top. The spirits are then forced to the top of the tank where they are sprayed over the fruit and slowly drip back to the bottom. This process is repeated many times until the maximum amount of flavor has been extracted from the fruit and mixed with the spirits.

Maceration is like brewing tea. The fruit or other flavoring agent is placed directly into a tank with the spirits for varying lengths of time.

After the flavors have been extracted by one of these two methods, the heavily flavored spirits are redistilled. The result is a distinct delicate flavor.

In distillation, the leaves, seeds, or flowers are placed in a still, then covered with a spirit and distilled. The final distillate will carry the flavor of the ingredients used. The finished product has a high alcohol content. Its high proof is reduced by the addition of a non-flavored syrup. Some manufacturers will use only this method of distillation.

Many of the same general types of liqueurs are produced by different distilling companies. Although they will all be similar in flavor, each will be slightly different because of the method, care, and amount of ingredients used.

Liqueurs can be broken down into five distinct categories: fruits, seeds, herbs, peels, and cremes. They are all unique and have very special flavors.

Fruits are the most popular category. The liqueurs will be plainly labeled with the name of the fruit used. Favorite fruit flavored liqueurs are Midori, made from melons, CocoRibe, made from coconuts, and Peter Heering, made from cherries.

Although most seed-based liqueurs don't use a single seed, they use a variety of ingredients, and one seed flavor will predominate.

In the herb category, no single herb will stand out, except for those made from mint or aniseed. This group uses a combination of herbs and sometimes seeds and flowers. Chartreuse is said to contain over 125 different ingredients. A large majority of these liqueurs are sold under well known trade names, and are made from secret formulas that have been passed down through the ages.

Peels are frequently given the name of the flavor from the rind of the citrus fruit used. One of the most widely used peel is that of the West Indian Curacao orange.

The most popular of the cremes is creme de menthe, which is the essence of mint. The mint is extracted in a colorless form, which is called white or clear creme de menthe. Sometimes green or gold coloring is added to give drinks an extra appeal, such as a Grasshopper. With color being their only difference, they all taste the same. (There is also no difference in taste between dark and white creme de cacao.) "Creme de" is French for "cream of," and is indicative of the creamy texture and sweet taste of these liqueurs. Cremes will take on the name of the dominant ingredient, such as banana, cocoa, coffee, etc. They are usually sweeter than other cordials, and are primarily used in mixed drinks, except for green creme de menthe which is frequently served straight or over crushed ice.

18 LIQUEUR REFERENCE

Abisante Anise flavored, pale green, substitute for absinthe

Abrictos, Creme d', or Abricotine An apricot liqueur from France

Absinthe Anise flavored, made with wormwood; illegal in most countries

Advokaat An eggnog liqueur, originally from Holland

Akvavit (Aquavit) Made from rye and caraway, originally from Scandanavia

Allasch Cumin flavored

Almond, Creme d' Made from almonds and sometimes other fruit pits. Substitute for creme de noyaux.

Almondrado An almond liqueur with a tequila base, produced in Mexico

Amaretto Almond flavored, made from apricot pits. The original is Amaretto di Saronno, made in Italy. Now, other distillers are producing their versions.

Ambrosia A Canadian liqueur

Amer Picon An aperitif from France, made from quinine, oranges, and gentian

Anise; Anisette; Anesone Licorise flavored, made from anise seeds

Apple Flavored Brandy An apple liqueur

Apricot Liqueur; Apry; Creme d' Abricots; Abricotine All are made from apricot pits

B & B Brandy and Benedictine blended

Banana Liqueur; Bananes, Creme d' Banana flavored

Benedictine Brandy based, combined with sugar, plants, and herbs such as hyssop, mint, and melissa—twenty-seven altogether. Discovered by Benedictine monks in France. Only two monks know this carefully guarded secret formula. The letters D.O.M. on the label stand for Deo

Optimo Maximo, "to God, most good, most great."

Ben Shalom An orange liqueur from Israel

Blackberry Liqueur Made from blackberries

Cacao, Creme d' (Brown and White) Cacao (chocolate) based, with vanilla beans

Cafe Benedictine A blend of Benedictine and coffee liqueur

Cafe, Creme de Made from coffee beans

Cafe Orange A blend of coffee and orange liqueurs

Calisay Quinine flavored, medium sweetness; made in Spain

Cassis, Creme de Made from French black currants

Cerise, Creme de A French cherry liqueur

Chartreuse (Yellow, 80 and 86 proof; Green, 110 proof) Brandy based, with plants and approximately 130 herbs; spicy and aromatic, made in France

Cheri-Suisse Flavored with chocolate and cherries

Cherry Heering A Danish cherry liqueur

Cherry Blossom Liqueur A very light cherry-flavored Japanese liqueur

Cherry Marnier A French cherry liqueur, with a hint of almond

Cherry Rocher A French cherry liqueur, true in flavor

Cherry Vanilla Predominantly cherry flavored, with vanilla added

Choclair coconut and chocolate flavored, with some herbs, from the United States

Chococo Coconut and chocolate flavored, from the Virgin Islands

CocoRibe A blend of coconut and rum

Coffee Liqueur Derived from coffee beans

Coffee Sambuca A blend of coffee liqueur and Sambuca

Cognac and Orange A blend of triple-distilled orange liqueur and cognac

Cointreau A product of France, made by maceration and double distillation of bitter and sweet orange peels. Substitute for triple sec

Cordial Medoc From France, a blend of oranges, cherries, brandy, and creme de cacao

Cranberry Liqueur Made from cranberries

Curacao Made from the peels of Curacao oranges. Comes in blue, white, green, and orange colors, all tasting the same. Substitute for triple sec

Drambuie Scotch-based liqueur with heather, honey, and herbs added. It was the liqueur of Prince Charles Edward.

Fior di Alpi; Fiore d' Alpe; Flora di Alpi; Flora Alpina All are different names for an Italian liqueur made from herbs and spices. The bottle contains a twig covered with crystallized sugar.

Forbidden Fruit An apple liqueur

Fraises, Creme de; Fraisette A strawberry liqueur

Framboise, Creme de A raspberry liqueur

Galliano Anise and vanilla flavored, made in Italy

George M. Tiddy's Canadian Liqueur Citrus flavored, with a medium sweetness

Glayva Scotch based, flavored with honey, anise, and herbs

Goldwasser, Danziger; Gold Liqueur Orange-herbal flavored liqueur with specks of gold leaf in it

Grand Marnier Cognac based, orange flavored; produced in France

Hungarian Pear Liqueur Derived from pears

Irish Mist Irish whisky based, flavored with honey and orange

Kahlua A coffee liqueur, flavored with vanilla; made in Mexico

Kirsch, Creme de; Kirschwasser Liqueur Made from sweet white cherries; conversely, Kirschwasser is a dry white brandy

Kummel Caraway flavored

Lochan Ora Scotch based and flavored with herbs, Lochan Ora means "Golden Lake"

Mandarine Cognac based, flavored with tangerines

Maraschino Cherry and almond flavored

Menthe, Creme de (White, Green, Pink, Gold) Derives its flavor from mint leaves, plus a hint of menthol

Midori A honeydew melon flavored liqueur from Japan

Moka, Creme de A coffee liqueur

Noyaux, Creme de, or Creme de Noya Predominantly almond flavored, made from the pits of plums, cherries, peaches, and apricots. A substitute for creme de almond

Ouzo Greek anise-flavored aperitif liqueur

Parfait Amour The name means "Perfect Love." Flavored with lemon, coriander, anisette, vanilla, orange, flowers, and a variety of other ingredients

Pasha A Turkish coffee liqueur

Passion Fruit Liqueur Flavor of either peach or mango, from Hawaii

Peach Liqueur Brandy or neutral spirit based, with fresh peaches or fresh and dried mixed

Peanut Lolita Made from peanuts

Pear Liqueur From pears, made in Hungary. Williams Pear Liqueur has a whole pear in the bottle, which makes an interesting conversation piece.

Peppermint Schnapps A mint liqueur, with a higher proof than creme de menthe

Pernod Licorice flavored

Peter Heering A Danish cherry liqueur

Pineapple Liqueur; Licor de Pina; Creme d'Ananas Pure pineapple flavor, from the Caribbean or Hawaii

Pistachio Liqueur; Pistasha Pistachio nut flavor

Prunella; Prunelle, Creme de Predominantly plum flavored, sometimes blended with prunes, figs, and vanilla

Raki Anise flavored liqueur from the Middle East

Raspberry Liqueur; Framboise Made from fresh or wild raspberries

Rock and Rye Rye whisky, mixed with rock-candy syrup and fruit juices. Slices of fruit are in the bottle. One type has crystallized sugar instead of fruit.

Roiano Anise and vanilla flavored, from Italy

Ron Coco Rum and coconut flavored

Rose, Creme de Made from vanilla and spices, and has the aroma of rose petals

Sabra Chocolate and orange flavored, from Israel

Sambuca Made from the sambuca plant which has a licorice (anise) flavor, produced in Italy

Sciarada Orange and lemon flavored, from Italy

Sloe Gin Made from sloeberries (sloe plums) of the black-thorn bush

Southern Comfort From New Orleans, it is whisky based and flavored with peaches

Strawberry Liqueur Derived from strawberries. If imported, it is called Fraise or Fraise de Bois (wild strawberries).

Strega Made from many herbs and spices, it is very similar to Galliano, and is also from Italy.

Swedish Punsch Rum based, with spices and citrus flavors. It is also known as Caloric Punsch.

Tia Maria Made from Blue Mountain coffee beans and spices, produced in Jamaica

Triple Sec Orange flavored, almost identical to Curacao

Tuaca Brandy based, with citrus flavors. Since milk is an ingredient, it is also known as "milk brandy." It is made in Italy.

Vaklova Vodka based, flavored with herbs

Van der Mint Dutch chocolate-mint liqueur

Vanilla, or Vanilla, Creme de From the Caribbean, made from vanilla beans

Violette, Creme de; Yvette, Creme de Made from violet petals and spices

Wild Turkey Liqueur Bourbon based, lightly flavored with spices

Yukon Jack Canadian whisky based, with citrus and herb flavors

DRINK INDEX

YOUR OWN DRINKS

YOUR OWN DRINKS

YOUR OWN DRINKS

YOUR OWN DRINKS

YOUR OWN DRINKS

_____

_____

_____

_____

_____

_____

_____

_____

_____

_____

_____

_____

_____

_____

_____

_____

_____